*The Neglected Walt Whitman*
VITAL TEXTS

# The Neglected Walt Whitman

## VITAL TEXTS

EDITED AND INTRODUCED BY
## SAM ABRAMS

**FOUR WALLS EIGHT WINDOWS**
*New York/London*

Much I owe to many dear friends and mentors,
But more, far more than to all the rest together,
To Barbara

A Four Walls Eight Windows First Edition
Introduction, notes, and selection copyright © 1993 by Sam Abrams
Published by Four Walls Eight Windows
P.O. Box 548, Village Station, New York, N.Y. 10014
First printing April 1993

Library of Congress Cataloging-in-Publication Data
Whitman, Walt, 1819-1892.
The neglected Walt Whitman/edited by Sam Abrams.—1st ed.
p. cm.
ISBN 0-941423-90-5 (cloth)/ ISBN 0-941423-97-2 (paper)
1. Abrams, Sam. 2. Title.
PS3204 1993
811' 3—dc20          92-42579
CIP

Photo credits: Front cover portraits of Whitman (clockwise from upper
left corner): 1. Gabriel Harrison, c. 1854. The William D. Bayley
Collection, Beeghly Library, Ohio Wesleyan University. 2. photographer
unknown, c. 1864. The William D. Bayley Collection, Beeghly Library,
Ohio Wesleyan University. 3. Matthew Brady, c. 1862. Walt Whitman
Collection, Clifton Waller Barrett Library, Special Collections
Department, University of Virginia Library. 4. J. Gurney and Son, 1871.
The William D. Bayley Collection, Beeghly Library, Ohio Wesleyan
University. 5. Thomas Eakins, 1891. The National Portrait Gallery,
Smithsonian Institution. 6. Thomas Eakins, 1891. Hirshhorn Museum and
Sculpture Garden, Smithsonian Institution, Transferred from Hirshhorn
Museum and Sculpture Garden Archives, 1983. 7. photographer unknown,
1871.The William D. Bayley Collection, Beeghly Library, Ohio Wesleyan
University. 8. J. Gurney and Son, c. 1870s. Walt Whitman Collection,
Clifton Waller Barrett Library, Special Collections Department,
University of Virginia Library. Center: Matthew Brady, c. 1862. Walt
Whitman Collection, Clifton Waller Barrett Library, Special Collections
Department, University of Virginia Library. Back cover portrait of
Whitman: George C. Cox, 1887. National Portrait Gallery, Smithsonian
Institution. The Carpenter Portrait of Whitman, page 42: Samuel Hollyer,
c. 1854-1855. National Portrait Gallery, Smithsonian Institution.

Printed in the U.S.A.

# Table of Contents

*Date of first publication and, where a second date has been added (**), of final major revision.

# Introduction

The Americans are not worthy of their Whitman.

—D.H. Lawrence

Walt Whitman is our greatest poet, our most American poet, our most international poet, a world-historical figure, the first modern, the first post-modern. Nobel Prize winner Pablo Neruda pronounced the world's verdict: "We live in a Whitmanesque Age." But America— official America, "mainstream," establishment America—was slow to honor our native bard. Even today when all critics acknowledge his fundamental importance, there is no edition for the general reader that contains all of his most significant poetry and prose. The most widely circulated readers' editions, such as those of the Library of America and Modern Library, by their omissions, seriously misrepresent Whitman as a much less radical thinker and much less conscious artist than he in fact was. This volume is intended to remedy that lack and to make the most frequently neglected of Whitman's *essential* works accessible to the general reader so that you may have the opportunity to encounter, on your own, Whitman

1

entire, in all his contrarieties, the unsafe Whitman, Whitman the subversive.

> I give you fair warning before you attempt me
> further,
> I am not what you supposed but far different.
>
> Who is he that would become my follower?
>
> The way is suspicious, the result uncertain,
> perhaps destructive.
> ("Whoever you Are Holding me Now in Hand")

This volume contains 66 texts which are essential for any serious encounter with Walt Whitman: 49 poems, 11 passages from poems, four prose texts, and one image-text. Some of these are *absolutely crucial* (and are so recognized by the overwhelming consensus of contemporary critics) for comprehending the radicality, the complexity and the sheer artistry of Whitman's poetic achievement. Others are equally crucial for illuminating the great sexual mystery of Whitman's biography, and, even more importantly for throwing light on the tangled relationship between the "real" Walt Whitman (1819-1892) and the immortal persona he created in *Leaves of Grass*—"Walt Whitman, a kosmos."

Currently available readers' editions are all seriously incomplete. In spite of repeated and emphatic testimonies by critics and poets to the centrality of the texts contained in this volume, *most* readers' editions of

Whitman omit *most* of these texts; *all* readers' editions omit *some* of them; *some* editions omit *all* of them. The "authoritative" Library of America *Complete Poetry and Collected Prose*, which aspires to become the standard Whitman "for generations" lacks all these vital texts. The Library's recently issued edition of *Leaves of Grass* adds some of the neglected texts, but it omits such important poems as "Pictures" and all those in the Old Age Echoes group, as well as all the collected prose. Meanwhile the LofA's *Complete Poetry and Collected Prose* is so incomplete that if it were a breakfast cereal, the FDA would demand recall or relabeling.

But now, finally, with this volume plus the Library of America's, the reader can have available all of Whitman's most important prose and poetic works in reasonably convenient form. With these texts in hand the reader will have full access to the two aspects of Whitman's life and work that the poet sought to conceal, or, at least, obscure: his commitment to male-male sexual love, and, most surprisingly, an intense negativity, a furious indignation, profoundly doubtful of the entire democratic experiment. Among the texts in this volume you will find the two very rarely printed poems "Calamus 8" and "Calamus 9," two most intensely personal poems from the sequence in which Whitman celebrated "the manly love of comrades." Also here is the tremendously important, suppressed poem "Respondez!," which in its ferocious denunciation of a society debased past redemption is matched to my knowledge by nothing in world literature but the Book of Jeremiah.

"Respondez!" is quite simply essential; it is the only poem in which Whitman reveals to us the profound discontent which underlies his perennial optimism.

Why is it that poems as important as "Respondez!" and the Calamus pair are so hard to find? I, who loved Whitman from boyhood, did not come to "Respondez!" until my 35th year. I remember the shock. It was 1962. I was reading Louis Zukofsky's "Five Statements for Poetry," in the latest issue of the very avant-garde little magazine *Kulcher.* (II, 8, 82) In his abrupt, paratactic way, Zukofsky suddenly cited what he introduced as "Whitman's greatest poem." There followed the whole text of "Respondez!." I sat stunned. How could I have missed it in 23 years of reading Whitman?

There are two "reasons," two sets of phenomena that explain why the readers' editions of Whitman are so inadequate.

First there are the obstacles created by Whitman himself. We can call it, following Gay Wilson Allen, The Magic Tree Problem. The very essence of Whitman's poetic project/process created complex questions and ambiguities that present a uniquely difficult challenge to any editor: misdirections, ambiguities, complications—traps for inadvertence or indifference. In 35 years of work on his book, Whitman issued around (!) nine (some scholars count ten, some eight) books called *Leaves of Grass*, each of them differing in its contents: six were major revisions. Few, if any, poets have rewritten as continuously as Whitman; none as publicly. He even seems to have lost count of the revisions of *Leaves* himself, describing the final edition as the "result of seven or eight stages and struggles." From the first (1855) edition of 95 pages containing 12 poems to the "death-bed edition" of 289 poems on 438 pages, the development of *Leaves* is a grandly organic spectacle, an evolutionary drama. The growth of the book is often (and very properly) read as a quasi-biological process, akin to maturation, metamorphosis. Thus, Gay Wilson Allen:

> The metaphor "growth" has often been applied to the work, and is perhaps the best descriptive term to use, but even assuming that many branches have died, atrophied, been pruned away, and new ones grafted on, the metaphor is still not entirely accurate—unless we think of a magical tree that bears different fruit in different seasons, now oranges, now lemons, occasionally a fragrant pomegranate. Not only by indefatigable revising, deleting, expanding, but also by constant re-sorting and rearranging the poems through six editions did Whitman indicate his shifting poetic intentions. Thus each of the editions and issues has its own distinctive form, aroma, import, though nourished by the same sap.
>
> (*Handbook* 67-8)

In training his magic tree, Whitman was not only concerned to present his fruits at their best and to clarify the interrelationships, he also artfully pruned so as to conceal, or shadow certain aspects of his work and of his life. Partly for obvious pragmatic reasons of self-preservation in one of the most prudish of known societies, partly for poetic reasons, Whitman, cutting, rewriting, and rearranging, hid completely or obscured and deemphasized what in earlier editions of *Leaves* had been explicit or prominent.

Although there is enough in any edition of *Leaves*, including the final edition, that testifies to Whitman's valuing of male-male sexual love (for instance "Recorders Ages Hence"), nevertheless, throughout his career, Whitman took pains to veil his homo-eroticism. In the 1860 (3rd) edition of *Leaves*, the celebration of homo-eroticism in a highly autobiographical mode reaches its clearest expression, but even in that most "outed" of the editions, he performed a camouflaging sex change in "Once I Passed through a Populous City." All Whitman's published versions of the poem portray a female lover, but Whitman's manuscript (*UPP* 11, 102) reads

> Once I pass'd through a populous city
> > imprinting my brain for future use with its
> > shows, architecture, customs, traditions.
> But now of all that city I remember only the
> > man who wandered with me there, for love
> > of me,
> Day by day and night by night we were
> > together—all else has long been forgotten
> > by me,

I remember, I say, only one rude and ignorant man.

In spite of that specific closeting, no one, from the perspective of the late 20th century, can argue that Whitman conceals or hides his passionate assent to male-male love in any edition of *Leaves*. Rather, he misdirects, much as a deer does, when, standing still, at the edge of the clearing, in the dappling, it lets the variegated pattern of light and shadow break the silhouette to fool the untrained eye. (But a small shift in perspective and you wonder, "How could I have missed it?")

What Whitman did take pains to well and truly expunge from later editions of *Leaves*, he succeeded in masking deeply. Consider this passage:

> With unprecedented materialistic advancement—society, in these States is cankr'd, crude, superstitious and rotten...What penetrating eye does not everywhere see through the mask? The spectacle is appalling. The men believe not in the women, nor the women in the men...The depravity of the business classes of our country is not less than has been supposed but infinitely greater. The official services of America, national, state and municipal, in all their branches and departments, except the judiciary, are saturated in corruption, bribery, falsehood, mal-administration; and the judiciary is tainted. The great cities reek

with respectable as much as non-respectable robbery and scoundrelism.

Who is that? Our Walt, the praise-singer of Democracy? The Good Gray Poet? It sounds like some alienated rebel or frustrated reformer. Jacob Riis? Orestes Brownson? Gene Debs? Garrison? Godkin of *The Nation*? Indeed it is Whitman; the passage is deeply buried in the too little read prose book *Democratic Vistas*, and was written in 1870.

This deeply pessimistic, critical view of post-Civil War America was, of course, shared by Mark Twain (*The Gilded Age*) and Henry Adams (*Democracy*). The moralizing fervor of the passage above seems to echo Thomas Nast's scathing Tweed Ring cartoons, which were appearing in *Harper's Weekly* at the very time that Whitman was composing *Democratic Vistas*. But this deeply subversive negativism is what Whitman, finally, refused to allow poetic expression in *Leaves of Grass*. After including his withering "Respondez!" in five editions of *Leaves*, in a heroic act of artistic discipline, he suppressed the great poem in 1881 so as to leave unblotched his created vision of "These States...the amplest poem" that animates *Leaves of Grass*.

Thus, with two great themes that he deemphasized or obscured, and with a score of themes that he rearranged and reharmonized in "seven or eight" version of *Leaves*, Whitman left the conscientious editor with Gordian tangles, an embarrassment of choices.[1]

The other reason why we still lack a truly comprehensive readers' Whitman is that, until relatively recently, the American academic establishment rejected and devalued Whitman to an extent that is hard to credit in retrospect. The American cultural elite has just got around to acknowledging Whitman, and are still rejecting and devaluing him, only in new ways.

In 1921, D.H. Lawrence, in *Studies in Classic American Literature*, could see Whitman for what he is:

> The one man breaking a way ahead. Whitman,
> the one pioneer. And only Whitman. No
> English pioneers, no French. No European
> pioneer-poets. In Europe the would be pioneers are mere innovators. The same in
> America. Ahead of Whitman, nothing. Ahead
> of all poets, pioneering into the wilderness of
> unopened life, Whitman. (183)

Yet, in his own land, no prophet with less honor. Whitman was repudiated, marginalized by the American cultural establishment, that Cambridge crew. And this rejection continued well into our century. "We live in a Whitmanesque age," but Bliss Carmen's 1925 *Oxford Book of American Verse*, which was reprinted through the 1940s, gave almost twice as much space to Longfellow as to Whitman. F.O. Matthiessen was the author of the enormously influential critical study *The American Renaissance* (1941), which finally established Whitman's classic status beyond cavil. In the 1930s,

Matthiessen, then a graduate student at Harvard, wanted to write his Ph.D. thesis on Whitman, and was refused permission on the grounds that there was nothing of substantial interest in the proposed subject.

Whitman anticipated it all. When he presented his claim on America's affection, it was with the clear expectation that his account would be long overdue before it was honored.

> Give me the pay I have served for...
> I have loved the earth, sun, animals, I have
>     despised riches,
> I have given alms to every one that ask'd,
>     stood up for the stupid and crazy, devoted
>     my income and labor to others,
> Hated tyrants, argued not concerning God,
>     had patience and indulgence toward the
>     people, taken off my hat to nothing known
>     or unknown,
> Gone freely with powerful uneducated persons
>     and with the young and with the mothers
>     of families,
> Read these leaves to myself in the open air,
>     tried them by trees, stars, rivers,
> Dismiss'd whatever insulted my own soul or
>     defiled my body,
> Claim'd nothing for myself which I have not
>     carefully claim'd for others on the same
>     terms...

I am willing to wait to be understood by the
   growth of the taste of myself.
                           ("By Blue Ontario's Shore")

The waiting was to last three generations. The polite
found Whitman's claims out of line and his services
irrelevant to what they understood as literature.
Whitman's rejection by the American cultural establish-
ment was accomplished with unusual cruelty, enough to
break any less imperturbable spirit. At first he was wel-
comed, indeed hailed, then ejected, marginalized,
ignored. It began in 1855. Whitman sent a copy of the
first (self-published) edition of *Leaves of Grass* to the
preeminent American literary man of the day, Ralph
Waldo Emerson, who responded with the most famous
literary letter of American history.

*Concord, Massachusetts, 21 July, 1855.*

Dear Sir,
I am not blind to the worth of the wonderful
gift of *Leaves of Grass*. I find it the most extra-
ordinary piece of wit and wisdom that America
has yet contributed. I am very happy in
reading it, as great power makes us happy. It
meets the demand I am always making of what
seemed the sterile and stingy Nature, as if too
much handiwork or too much lymph in the
temperament were making our western wits
fat and mean.

I give you joy of your free and brave thought. I have great joy in it. I find incomparable things said incomparably well, as they must be. I find the courage of treatment, which so delights us, and which large perception only can inspire.

I greet you at the beginning of a great career, which yet must have had a long foreground somewhere, for such a start. I rubbed my eyes a little to see if this sunbeam were no illusion; but the solid sense of the book is a sober certainty. It has the best merits, namely, of fortifying and encouraging.

I did not know until I, last night, saw the book advertised in a newspaper, that I could trust the name as real and available for a postoffice. I wish to see my benefactor, and have felt much like striking my tasks, and visiting New York to pay you my respects.

R.W. Emerson

This grand, generous gesture marked the high water mark of Whitman's acceptance; it was followed by a long and drastic ebb. At first attracted, Emerson and the rest of the reputable literati, as they realized the intractibility of Whitman's radicalism, retreated, silently oozing away. The low water mark was reached in 1876, on the centennial of these States, that year of the most openly corrupt American presidential election, year of the death of Reconstruction, year of the birth of Jim

Crow. Whitman, who had so often identified his fate
with that of the American experiment, who had pub-
lished the first *Leaves* on the Fourth of July, now
seemed, in Gilded Age America, as marginal and futile
as his democratic idealism. He had been hard hit by a
triple rejection. Between 1870 and 1875, three "major"
American poetry anthologies appeared, each claiming to
define the canon of the "great" and "best," each edited
by a "major" New England poet: William Cullen
Bryant's *Library of Poetry and Song*, the immensely
respected Emerson's *Parnassus*, and John Greenleaf
Whittier's *Songs of Three Centuries*. None of these three
prestigious volumes included any work by Walt
Whitman. What, after all that, was Whitman feeling as
he launched the "Centennial" Edition of his *Leaves*?

> 1876 was a critical and turning point in my
> personal and literary life. [I published] the
> *Leaves*...some home customers for them, but
> mostly from the British Islands. I was seriously
> paralyzed, poor, in debt, was expecting death,
> (the doctors put four chances out of five
> against me). Curiously, the sale abroad proved
> prompt and...copious: the names came in lists
> and the money with them. Both the cash and
> the emotional cheer were deep medicines;
> many paid double or treble the price,
> (Tennyson and Ruskin did,) and many sent
> kind and eulogistic letters; ladies, clergymen,
> social leaders, persons of rank, and high offi-

cials. Those blessed gales from the British Islands probably (certainly) saved me. Here are some of the names, for I w'd like to preserve them: Wm. M. and D.G. Rossetti, Lord Houghton, Edwd. Dowden, Mrs. Ann Gilchrist, Keningale Cook, Edwd. Carpenter, Therese Simpson, Rob't Buchanan, Alfred Tennyson, John Ruskin...

(*Some Personal and Old Age Jottings*)

The list goes on for sixty names, inevitably reminding us of the names of American writers who are missing, who had abandoned and scorned Whitman: a long, silent roll of shame: Bryant, Whittier, Longfellow, Holmes, Dana, Emerson, Howells, even Henry James, who found Whitman's Civil War poems "melancholy reading." (It took James decades to learn better.)

"Give me the pay I have served for!" The blessed gales from the British Islands had saved him, but the big winds at home were contrary or still. Nor were they to change in his lifetime. In his last year, summing up, he wrote, "from a worldly and business point of view 'Leaves of Grass' has been worse than a failure—public criticism on the book and myself as author of it yet shows mark'd anger and contempt more than anything else."

It was to take another 65 years before the tide began to turn, with Matthiessen's *American Renaissance*; since then the current has run strong in his (our) favor.[2] In the late 1950s, when the populist post-modernistic waves finally rolled over the critical barriers erected in the name of High Modernism, Whitman, at last, achieved wide recognition as our pillar of fire, the one pioneer. Thus, the breakthrough post-modern book, Allen Ginsberg's *Howl*, bears on its title page, as keynote for the new age, these lines from *Song of Myself*:

> Unscrew the locks from the doors!
> Unscrew the doors themselves from their
> jambs![3]

Through the doorways came, and are still coming, the living crowds: the Beats, Bob Dylan, feminists, Mau-Mau Poets, The Velvet Underground, The Last Poets, Stand Up Poets, The Good Gay Poets, jazz poets, Black Mountaineers, neo-surrealists, confessional poets, Deep Imagists, Nuyoricans, Dial-a-Poet, Poetry Slams and all those diversely yawping vitalities.

> Rhymes and rhymers pass away, poems
>     distill'd from poems pass away,
> The swarms of reflectors and the polite pass,
>     and leave ashes,
> Admirers, importers, obedient persons, make
>     but the soil of literature,
> America justifies itself, give it time, no disguise
>     can deceive or conceal from it...
> If its poets appear it will in due time advance
>     to meet them, there is no fear of mistake.
>                     ("By Blue Ontario's Shore")

Nowadays, the decades of error seem forgotten and there is sufficiency of melodramatic praising: Whitman shopping centers and bridges, prizes and societies. In the ivied towers, ceremonious lip service. And quite a few truly useful scholarly studies. Now the grand viziers of critical opinion are on the job and pages of *The New York Times Book Review* and *The New York Review of Books* salute Whitman: "our greatest American poet" (Harvard Professor Vendler); "crucial to an American mythology...absolutely central to our literary culture" (Yale Professor Bloom).

Yet there are false notes. All is not sweet, all is not sound. A nation of homeowners, by their homes ye shall know them (see Thoreau's *Walden*). Whitman's working class house, he called it his "shanty," sits in rustbelt desolation in Camden. Barely maintained by the State of New Jersey and the efforts of the Whitman Association, it is still recognizably a poor person's house. While, on Brattle Street, Tory Row in Cambridge, the mansion of Longfellow, Brahmin Harvard professor, is maintained in official splendor as a national monument. Real property expressing real values. What can our elite do with a Whitman, who really did prefer to hang out with blue collar types, bubbas, street toughs, bag-people, rough trade, "powerful uneducated persons"? All his life. Never took to the writers' conference circuit. No polite person he. "Me, a Manhattanese, the most loving and arrogant of men." And his shanty announces it so clearly. It's hard for the professoriat to claim him as one of their own in sight of that gardenless, two-up, two-down rowhouse in dingy Camden, across from the jail. But no illusions are disturbed by a stroll in the extensive, curated gardens of the Longfellow Mansion.

*Deuteronomy* resonates: "And thou shalt write these words upon the doorposts of thy house and upon thy gates." And we do, willy-nilly, unconsciously, automatically, in spite of ourselves, irrevocably, for all to see. There we shall enshrine that which we serve with all heart and with all soul, to whose commandments we harken diligently. The tale of the houses. It is hard still for Americans of the literary establishment to look searchingly in Whitman's face, at his house, at his work. As his home is neglected and difficult of public access so is his complete text.

Thus, one hundred years after his death, although we have an academic Whitman industry complete with trade organization and journal, we still have no truly comprehensive *readers'* edition of our classic poet. We do have *scholars'* editions. The needs of the studious are served by the many, large volumes of the NYU Press *Collected Writings* and its offshoots such as the "Norton Critical" *Leaves of Grass*. But these editions are not what Whitman wanted; they are irrelevant to the audience he addresses.

> In any roof'd room I emerged not...
> And in libraries I lie as one dumb, a gawk, or
>     unborn, or dead
> ...Thrusting me beneath your clothing

> Where I may feel the throbs of your heart or
>     rest upon your hip,
> Carry me when you go forth over land or sea.
>     ("Whoever You Are Holding Me Now in Hand")

My hopes were high that, at last, we would have a Whitmanesque edition of Whitman when, in 1982, the Library of America, issued its first four volumes, among them the *Complete Poetry and Collected Prose of Walt Whitman* edited by Justin Kaplan. The Library of America is a nonprofit undertaking, funded by the National Endowment for the Humanities and the Ford Foundation, with a board of literary and scholarly superstars. Jason Epstein seems to be, in effect, the CEO, actively setting policy in his position as Treasurer of The Literary Classics of United States, Inc., the not-for-profit corporate parent of the Library of America. Epstein is one of the great names in American publishing. In the '50s he started the paperback revolution with the first successful line of "quality" (now called "trade") literary paperbacks; he was a founder of *The New York Review of Books*, and now holds the position of editorial director of many-mansioned Random House. The Library of America purports to be the fulfillment of Edmund Wilson's long campaign, a mission Wilson passed on in a letter to Epstein.

> Dear Jason: I am glad to hear that you are going to take up...the possibility of bringing out in a complete and compact form the prin-

cipal American classics. I have, as you know, been trying for years to interest some publisher in the project. It is absurd that our most read and studied writers should not be available in their entirety in any convenient form. The kind of thing I should like to see would follow the example of the *Editions de la Pléiade*, which have included the whole of the French classics in beautifully produced...thin paper volumes. (*Letters* 684)

The Library of America, in its publicity and in its grant applications, has defined its mission as publishing "the classics of American literature in authoritative and durable editions, the best possible modern editions, responsibly edited editions, that will last for generations." And when the Library of America's *Complete Poetry and Collected Prose* of Walt Whitman (*CPCP*) appeared, the reviewers, with no dissent, agreed: the "most comprehensive edition of his work to date," "the most complete one volume edition ever." But the volume was, in fact, disappointing in regard to both of Wilson's criteria: it was neither complete nor compact.

As soon as I saw it and hefted it I was disappointed. It is no backpacker's edition, no mountain climber's. Way too bulky, way too heavy. (Of all the reviewers, Hugh Kenner alone, in *Harper's*, noted the unhandy size, and its anti-Whitmanian significance.) The volumes, though plain and handsome, without fins, are sized as classic Detroit gas guzzlers to the sleek Pléiade

Citroens. A Pléiade volume will fit (I have tried) in the outside pocket of a giveaway flight bag, in a tweed jacket's side pocket, in the back pockets of Levi's. The Library of America's volumes run about twice as fat as the Pleiades, about two inches to one, and about an inch taller, eight inches to seven. They are larger and stiffer enough so that they cannot be conveniently carried on one's person, heavier enough so that it is unpleasant to hold them in hand. The Library of America *CPCP* will not even fit in the side bellows pockets of my mountain parka, into which I can get *two* Pléiades, or the *Oxford Book of Greek Verse* plus *A Field Guide to the Birds*. And it weighs more than twice as much as a Pléiade!

Perhaps for some authors portability is no big deal but it was for Whitman, who, in his conversation, as in his poems, made his wishes clear. "I want no autocrat editions. All my own tastes are towards books you can handle easily—put into your pocket." (*Teller* 42)

> I tramp a perpetual journey...
> My signs are a rain-proof coat, good shoes and
>     a staff cut from the woods.
>                                   ("Song of Myself")

And no two-pounder books in my knapsack. Please. The physical bloat problem alone renders the volume useless for me. (Could it be motivated as anti-shoplifting device? Retail security is a boom industry in America.)

But, by far, the important failure of this professedly "authoritative" edition is its incompleteness. This is an especially grave problem because the Library of America *CPCP* aspires to be and is in fact achieving considerable acceptance as the "standard" Whitman; not uncommonly nowadays, it is the only edition cited in both scholarly and popular books[4]. Yet by any objective standard it is seriously, shockingly incomplete.

In *CPCP*, Kaplan tried to deal with The Magic Tree Problem by including the complete texts of the first (1855) *Leaves* and the final 1891-92 "deathbed" edition. The 1891-92 version is Whitman's final authorized edition, the considered product of 35 years laboring. He made his authorial intentions as clear as possible, with this note on the copyright page.

> As there are now several editions of L. of G., different texts and dates, I wish to say that I prefer and recommend this present one, complete, for future printing, if there should be any; a copy and facsimile, indeed of these 483 pages.

After completing the "deathbed" edition, Whitman, in conversations with his literary executor Horace Traubel, further clarified his intentions both for the future of *Leaves* and for any poems he might write in the short time he knew he had left. These last poems were collected in an "annex," under the title Whitman had prepared in advance, "Old Age Echoes" and published in the first posthumous edition of *Leaves of Grass* (1897). In "An Executor's Diary Note" (full text on page 45 below), Traubel, who for many years had been recording Whitman's conversation, passes on the poet's very precise instructions, both for "Old Age Echoes" and for the poems dropped from various editions of *Leaves*. Whitman concedes that he cannot prevent "the world" from reprinting these leaves "dropped by the roadside" some day, but places on Traubel (and responsible future editors) "the injunction that whatever may be added to the [458 pages of the 1891-92] *Leaves* shall be supplementary, avowed as such, [marked off by] an unmistakable, deep down, unobliterable division line." Seems clear enough.

With Whitman's intentions thus explicitly defined, with the Magic Tree casting its convoluted shadows, what does Kaplan give us in *CPCP*? For poetry, for a "Complete Poetry" he prints:

> —The 1891-92 authorized "deathbed" edition of *Leaves*, with the two annexes Whitman added during his lifetime, "Sands at Seventy" and "Good-bye My Fancy,"
> —The 1855 first edition of *Leaves*,
> —The few poems Whitman placed into his 1892 *Complete Prose Works*.

This is all very well as far as it goes. The inclusion of the 1855 text has been widely and correctly praised as Kaplan's best editorial decision. Almost all modern critics have followed Malcolm Cowley in judging the 1855 to be the most important early edition of *Leaves*.

Cowley, indeed, even argued that it is more authentic than Whitman's final revision and campaigned for forty years to establish his view:

> "The text of the first edition is the purest text for 'Song of Myself' since many of the later corrections were also corruptions of style and concealments of meaning...it is likewise the best text for most of the other poems...[it] is a unified work, unlike any later edition."
> (*Handbook* 81, *Cowley Introduction* x)[5]

Kaplan's inclusion of the 1855 text represents the vindication of Cowley's view and would have been entirely praiseworthy if only Kaplan had respected Whitman's instructions and placed the first edition as a supplement *after* the authorized 1891-92 text, "marked off by an unmistakable...division line." Giving the 1855 text pride of place, in the light of Whitman's clear authorial intention, seems remarkably insensitive—the triumph of Cowley's Whitman over Whitman's Whitman.

When we begin to consider the poems that Kaplan's selection omits and that this present volume contains, we find, at the very outset, a stunning repudiation of Whitman's authorial intention. Inexplicably missing is the undoubtedly canonic "Old Age Echoes" annex, in clear violation of the unambiguous, never doubted testimony of the "Executor's Diary Note" that Whitman fully intended it to be appended to future editions of *Leaves*. This is unparalleled. To disregard authorial intention for the sake of *inclusiveness* is widely accepted editorial practice, but to do so for the sake of *exclusion* from a "Complete Poetry" is, by any definition, irresponsible: disservice to readers, disrespect to author. I know of only one other case of omission of indubitably canonic poems from an edition issued by a reputable publisher. In the American issue (Harvard UP 1953) of the "Muses' Library" *Poems* of Lord Rochester, two famous pornographic poems were excluded. But, in that case, at least an editor's note sought to justify the cut "as owing to the risk of prosecution." In contrast, Kaplan, in his "Notes on the Texts," says absolutely nothing to explain his astonishing omission of "Old Age Echoes." Such silence strongly suggests that the omission was— unforgivably—sheer blunder.

Is there any other classic American author who has, continuously, received such shoddy treatment from the establishment? What is it about Whitman that the insiders keep trying to dodge? And isn't a blunder of this kind enough—by itself—to raise serious doubts about the editorial standards and procedures of the Library of America?

This present volume contains then, first, "Old Age Echoes," the third of the three annexes which Whitman added to *Leaves of Grass*, and which concludes with the last poem he wrote, "A Thought of Columbus." In these annexes, his powers are diminished, as he was the first to admit.

> In this old age and paralysis of me...getting
> stiffer and stuck deeper, much like some hard-

cased dilapidated shell-fish or time banged
conch...cast up high and dry on the shore-
sands, helpless to move anywhere.

(Preface Note to 2nd Annex)

But what isn't diminished is—what perhaps is most
essential to a poet—his sense of wonder at the world
and all it contains, and all it could contain. A child-lively
heart still dances to the world-music with "primal
buoyant centre-pulses down there deep somewhere
within his gray-blurr'd old shell." And the ancient, glit-
tering, gay eyes, peeking out from the shell, are still
capable of fresh noticings, as in, for instance, "The First
Dandelion."

> Simple and fresh and fair, from winter's close
>     emerging,
> As if no artifice of fashion, business, politics
>     had ever been.

And the battered sea-shell's voice, reverberant of the
great sea at full, faintly but genuinely oceanic, still sings
of love and of faith in love. "Of Many a Smutch'd Deed
Reminiscent" (page 51 below) belongs with the greatest
of Whitman's mini-madrigals. It is of the perfect strain
of "I Saw in Louisiana a Live-Oak Growing" and "I
Hear It Was Charged against Me." In his illness and old
age, a testament unparalleled, a gift outright.

In addition to leaving out "Old Age Echoes,"
Kaplan also omits all the poems that Whitman dropped

from intermediate editions of *Leaves*. By printing just the 1855 and 1891-92 texts, *CPCP* misses all the poems that Whitman added to the 1856, 1860, 1865, 1867, 1871, 1872, 1876 editions, but excised from the final *Leaves*. Whitman and Traubel (in "An Executor's Diary Note") specifically anticipated these poems being appended to *Leaves* someday.[6]

For these too, Whitman prepared an explicit decision in advance of his death, and it's posted, for all who care to see, in the "Executor's Note." When Traubel asked if Whitman put the dropped poems "under the ban"? Whitman replied, "Why should I?—how could I? [But] I place on you the injunction that whatever may be added to the *Leaves* shall be supplementary, avowed as such, leaving book complete as I left it, consecutive to the point that I left off." There exist 37 of these dropped poems, which Whitman published between 1856 and 1876, but decided not to include in the final *Leaves*. The Fallen Leaves I section of the present volume includes all the poems from the intermediate editions of *Leaves* that were cut from the final edition.

Of these, first in every sense is "Respondez!," which is quite simply one of Whitman's most important poems. This poem together with Whitman's suppression of it constitute a major key to reading *Leaves of Grass*.

> "These leaves and me you will not understand,
> They will elude you at first and still more
> afterwards."
> ("Whoever You Are Holding Me Now in Hand")

"Respondez!" first appeared in the 1856 *Leaves* under the title "Poem of the Propositions of Nakedness." Its last appearance in revised form was in the 1876 *Leaves*. The most important of its revisions are lines 2 and 17-20, which Whitman added in 1871; they have been called "the most blisteringly honest lines he wrote about the postwar nation." (*Thomas* 264)

The importance of the poem and of Whitman's decision to suppress it lie in that blistering honesty. Here alone in his poetry does Whitman address the America he saw all around him in the Gilded Age. There is nothing remotely comparable to it in his poetry. The only other sarcastic poem in his works is "A Boston Ballad," one of his earliest poems, which is indeed little like "Respondez!.". The sarcasm of the "Ballad" is directed against the behavior of a specific set of Americans in regard to a specific event, while the sarcasm of "Respondez!" is generalized, addressed universally to city and world.

> Let every one answer! let those who sleep be
> waked! let none evade!

This disembodied voice calling the damned to judgment—what could be more unexpected from Whitman? Perhaps the most marked characteristic of the Walt Whitman of *Leaves* is universal sympathy. For D.H. Lawrence this was the incomprehensible aspect of *Leaves*, the adhesive Whitman who embraces all, weaves all things into his self. And Emerson was specifically offended by the range of Whitman's sympathy in "To a Common Prostitute."

> Be composed—be at ease with me—I am Walt
> Whitman, liberal and lusty as Nature,
> Not till the sun excludes you do I exclude you,
> Not till the waters refuse to glisten for you and
> leaves to rustle for you, do my words refuse
> to glisten and rustle for you.

Only in "Respondez!," did Whitman allow poetic expression to the profound and general negativity that underlies the universal sympathy and idealized democracy which permeate *Leaves*. In Kenneth Burke's lapidary phrase, this was Whitman's "outlaw moment." Everywhere else in *Leaves*, as Burke puts it, "his futuristic idealizing could readily transform all apprehensions into promises, and could discern a unitary democratic spirit behind any aggregate." (*Burke* 293) But here alone all his doubts coalesce into a poem of extraordinary power, a poetic invective unique this side of the Old Testament prophets.

The knowledge that a Whitman existed capable of an expression so at variance with his optimistic vision of democracy perfected is of utmost importance to an understanding of his entire poetic project/process. Too often Whitman is read as a simplistic optimist, but his relentless idealizing strategy in *Leaves* gains new dimensions of meaning when read against the acute sense of

negativity so powerfully expressed in "Respondez!.."
From this poem we learn that, just as the Walt
Whitman of *Leaves of Grass* is a construction only some-
what resembling the "real" Walt Whitman, so the
America represented in *Leaves* as exultantly, athletically
ideal, that America he hears singing, is also a construc-
tion. The Whitman of *Leaves*, he who claims to never
doubt America ("The Union always swarming with
blatherers and always sure and impregnable.") not only
doubted, but, once, indeed, memorably vilified America,
*cursed* America, root and branch, cursed with all the
inspired vituperative force of a prophet of the angry
Jaweh. Paradoxically, "Respondez!" reinforces rather
than weakens our perception of Whitman's faith in
democracy. Only a profound belief can motivate so pro-
found a disappointment. Whitman rages because he,
like Jeremiah, is perfectly certain of his vision, and of
the capability of his fellows to realize that vision.

I cite just two of the many testimonies to the power
of this poem. In 1948, William Carlos Williams
received an invitation to address the elite English
Institute at Columbia University. Williams, clearly
appreciating the opportunity to lecture an audience of
distinguished academics on his passionate belief that
"poetic form *must* change," argued:

I think our one major lead, as Americans, is to
educe and exploit the significance of Walt
Whitman's formal excursions: *And nothing else!*

And as examples of Whitman's "great contribution...our major heritage from him," Williams recited passages from "Song of Myself" and almost the whole of "Respondez!." (*Williams* 65, 70-73)

Same location, Columbia, 21 years later, Saturday, April 27, 1968, we ("the people") surrounded Columbia University. It took tens of thousands of us, holding hands and singing—of course—"We Shall Overcome." A great and racially harmonious demo, "Black and White Together." (One of the last big integrated demos of the era. Still mourning Dr. King, two weeks in his grave.) The students had been occupying the campus since Tuesday, quite non-violently (all the eventual violence was by "New York's Finest"). The immediate issue was "Gym Crow." Columbia, one of the richest universities in the world, had contrived to grab a piece of Morningside Park, which serves one of the poorest communities in the country, Harlem. On this piece of park, Columbia was building a new gym, to which, the university administration adamantly proclaimed: no community access would be allowed. That was the trigger. The students had been sensitized by the Vietnam War and by Columbia's direct involvement in the dirtiest aspects of that war via the Institute for Defense Analysis, and by the university's racist real-estate enterprises. ("The great cities reek with respectable as much as non-respectable robbery and scoundrelism.") The occupiers sat on the window ledges over Broadway singing "We have Hamilton Hall in our hands, We have Grayson Kirk in our hands..." The citizens of Harlem applauded.[7] And, on a raw, cold Saturday, from all the five boroughs, we the people came, and surrounded the campus, and sang. Political and cultural "revolutionaries," poets, apparatchicks, yippies were passing out underground papers and leaflets. One of the most generally approved of those handouts was a broadside: Volume I, Number 4 of *Guerilla: the Newspaper of the Streets*, published by the "Center for Paleocybernetic Research" and the "Artists & Writers Militia" (no addresses given). Its lead text was Whitman's outlaw sermon "Respondez!." That's the Whitman whose help Neruda invoked in his last book, *Incitement to Nixoncide*. Whitman at his most subversive ("these leaves conning you con at peril").

Whitman's suppression of the poem is as revealing in its way as the poem itself. From the cutting of the poem—and how few poets could afford that cut!—we learn, in unmistakable terms, just how much of a conscious artist Whitman was. The "spontaneous me" fallacy is, of course, one that Whitman himself fostered. The distance between that crafted mask and the real patient craftsman is immense. There has never been a more conscious, a more painstaking craftsman than Whitman. After twenty years of refining it, finally, he sacrificed this magnificent poem for the sake of the organic whole. The scholar David Reynolds has recently emphasized how the "intensive negativity [of "Respondez!"] best represents Whitman's wholesale inversion of moral values...and is in fact the substratum for intense affirmations." (*Reynolds* 110-11, 521) Like any fine craftsman, Whitman concealed the substratum. Ironically, humanly, he couldn't, it seems, bring himself to entirely discard "Respondez!.." He left two little odd bits of it in the final *Leaves*, fragments really, probably the two most unrealized and inchoate passages in the entire book; they serve only as traces of the lost "Respondez!.." The placement of the six-line "Reversals" immediately after Whitman's definitive affirmation of democracy and poetry, "By Blue Ontario's Shore,"[8] seems significant, at least it does when the whole from which it is taken is known. Another scrap from "Respondez!" is placed right after "The Sleepers," to no apparent purpose that I can see; three lines long, it's titled "Transpositions." This imperfect excision is characteristically Whitmanesque and wonderfully apposite in the context of the "biological" growth process of *Leaves of Grass*. No tree, magical or mundane, loses major branches without leaving scars, nubbins, snags. That's why "Reversals" and "Transpositions" are the sort of imperfections you can find, if you look real close, marking every deep rooted, living blossomer.

After "Respondez!," the most significant of the dropped poems are the three from the "Calamus" cluster, which are included in the present volume. In 1860, Whitman was preparing the first commercial edition of *Leaves*, in which, in spite of Emerson's counsels of prudence, he decided to emphasize the "sex program" that he had announced in the letter to Emerson that had served as preface to the 1856 *Leaves*.

A word remains to be said, as of one ever present, not yet permitted to be acknowledged, discarded...by literature, and the results apparent. To the lack of an avowed, empowered, unabashed development of sex, (the only salvation for the same,)...is attributable the remarkable non-personality and indistinctness of modern productions in books, art, talk...savans, poets, historians, biographers, and the rest have long connived at the filthy law, and books enslaved to it, that what makes the manhood of a man, that sex, womanhood, maternity, desires, lusty animations, organs, acts, are unmentionable and to be ashamed of, to be driven to skulk out of literature...This filthy law has to be repealed.

One technique Whitman used, in the 1860 *Leaves*, to give sex its "avowed, empowered, unabashed development," was to group conspicuously both the heteroerotic and the homoerotic poems. The poems of male-female sexuality were gathered under the title "Enfans d' Adam" (in later editions changed to "Children of Adam"). It is here that Whitman placed the "Once I Passed through a Populous City" with the male lover of the manuscript made female. The homoerotic "Calamus" group was made up of 45 poems. It was here that Whitman, in the revisions of *Leaves*, intensified that dappling and mystifying shade to confuse the eyes of the unwary.

> Here the frailest leaves of me and yet my
>    strongest lasting,
> Here I shade and hide my thoughts, I myself
>    do not expose them,
> And yet they expose me more than all my
>    other poems.

By 1891, "Calamus" had been reduced to 39 poems. Calamus 8, 9 and 16, the three poems included in the present volume, Whitman suppressed entirely. Others he revised, others he moved around within the "Calamus" section, others he moved to different sections of *Leaves*. Calamus 8 and 9 were particularly valued by the Dane Frederick Schyberg, who was the first mainstream scholar to openly confront Whitman's homosexuality and its relevance to his poetry. He singled them out as "the two poems that disclosed most intimately and personally what had happened to him. [8] is absolutely astonishing. [9] is probably the most poignant love poem in the entire collection." (*Schyberg* 163-4) Probably, it is just because they are the most personally revealing of the series that Whitman removed them. Among his other disguising changes, he substituted the word "comrade" for the 1860 "lover" in the last poem in the sequence. Now, with the three texts included in this volume, it is possible to read "Calamus" in its original sequence, which cunningly reflects, by

direct, *almost* narrative, development, the private fore-
ground of these poems. (For the reader's convenience
and enjoyment of the entire Calamus group as a
sequence, the original order of the poems is charted in
the Appendix.)

The Fallen Leaves II and Manuscript Poems sections
include the most frequently cited and discussed of the
passages dropped from *Leaves* and the poems Whitman
never published. These are interesting primarily as
glimpses into Whitman's workshop, as antidotes to the
"spontaneous me" fallacy. Here we can sense the doing
and undoing, the patient artificing. Uniquely revealing
in this respect is the early poem, "Pictures," discovered
by Emory Holloway. It is famous as the one remaining
precursor of *Leaves of Grass*. Until Holloway discovered
it in 1925, the metamorphosis of Walter Whitman, the
journalist, the conventional man of letters into "Walt
Whitman, a kosmos" seemed an inexplicably sudden
transformation: hack to bard, jump cut. "Pictures" is a
window into what we now know was a laborious and
gradual process. Its discovery was a major stimulus to
the refocus of scholarly opinion that resulted in a
fruitful reexamination of Whitman's early years and
background.[9] Its great value for illuminating the actual
development, the working out of Whitman's poetic
innovations is immediately apparent. "Whitman's
embryonic verse," Holloway called it. Whitman was the
first to see that a modern, democratic poetry required a
*formal* revolution, a quantum leap into new verse

dimensions. In "Pictures," we witness the actual dis-
covery of modernism, the birth of a poetry rooted in the
uniqueness of individuals; we can hear Whitman finding
his voice. A voice that was used before it was under-
stood—the creative intuition in action, as always, pre-
ceding the definition. And Whitman listened to what he
had made and heard that it was good. As William Carlos
Williams insisted, "It is in the structure of the line that
the stasis of the thought is lodged!" (64) And it is in
"Pictures" that we can see (and hear!) Whitman, line by
line, word by word, pause by pause, working out a new
universe of poetic possibilities. Yet Kaplan left it out of
his "Complete Poetry," even though he had already
described it, in his Whitman biography, as a "decisive
preliminary study" for *Leaves of Grass* (*Kaplan* 153).

There are pleasures and surprises to be found
among these manuscript poems and fragments. Harold
Bloom's seemingly paradoxical insistence that "Wallace
Stevens and T.S. Eliot have in common...their hidden,
partially unconscious reliance upon Whitman as their
main predecessor" (*Bloom* 6) may seem an overstate-
ment. But compare the opening of "Poem of Existence"
with the opening of "Burnt Norton."

> We call one the past, and we call another the
>    future,
> But both are alike the present
> It is not the past, though we call it so,—nor
>    the future, though we call it so,

All the while it is the present only—both
   future and past are the present only.
                              ("Poem of Existence")


Time present and time past
Are both perhaps present in time future,
And time future contained in time past.
If all time is eternally present
All time is unredeemable.
                              ("Burnt Norton")


Is *Four Quartets*, at its unstill heartpoint, no more than an argument with Whitman?[10]


The only illustration included in the present volume is the so-called Carpenter Portrait, which I have selected for the frontispiece, as it was the frontispiece of the very first edition of *Leaves of Grass*. This image, shockingly revolutionary in its iconography in the context of Victorian America, was considered by Whitman an integral and essential part of *Leaves of Grass*. It is missing from *CPCP*. (That is not the only example of the Library of America depriving readers of illustrations which the authors had considered integral to their texts. Jack London's *People of the Abyss* was reprinted without the photographs, many taken by London himself.)

When this portrait first appeared facing the title page of the first edition of *Leaves*, there was no author's name on the title page itself. This outrageous figure,

radiating attitude, dressed like a menial laborer in fla-
grant violation of what all the world knew a poet should
look like, served as a signature of a special kind. This
image is a frontal challenge to the old (it goes back to
the Greeks) notion that poetry is the exclusive province
of the genteel. The portrait goes beyond the romantic
insistence on the divine poet; this is the divine poet who
takes out the trash. Here is the uncompromising bubba-
bard. Although, in the various editions of *Leaves*,
Whitman experimented with a range of images of him-
self, and, for some years dropped this flamboyant,
defiant portrait, in the final edition he restored the
Carpenter Portrait, placing it emphatically facing the
first page of "Song of Myself." A poet, an American
bard at last, has come, and come to stay, and he doesn't
give a damn for dress codes or any other anachronistic
vestiges of outmoded, class-bound anti-democratic
social theories. The portrait's message is clear, and in
1993 as timely as ever. Whitman *still* couldn't get into
the Harvard Club; no one can without a necktie, nor in
blue jeans.

The Uncollected Prose section in this book contains
three pieces of primary importance for critical apprecia-
tion of Whitman and one vivid autobiographical sketch.
In spite of their widely acknowledged significance, they
are all omitted by Kaplan. Indeed, nothing in
Whitman's prose has had a more profound influence on
our perceptions of his work than the two anonymous
1855 reviews and *An American Primer*. Whitman

reprinted and widely circulated these two self-reviews of the first edition of *Leaves*. They have been characterized as "an important extraliterary extension of *Leaves of Grass*, (*Greenspan* 98) and as "some of the most valuable biographical data in existence." (*Miller* 10) Almost every critic quotes, often prominently, as keynote the first of these reviews, which so vividly expresses Whitman's ambitions for his volume: "An American bard at last!"

*An American Primer*, a series of notes (which he worked on all his life) for a never delivered lecture on the American language, is the source for one of the most frequently quoted passages of Whitman's prose.

> A perfect writer would make words sing, dance, kiss, do the male and female act, bear children, weep, bleed, rage, stab, steal, fire cannon, steer ships, sack cities, charge with cavalry or infantry, or do anything that man or woman or the natural powers can do.

The *Primer*, pretty much throughout, is praeternaturally penetrating into the heart of this poetry business— words. Although Traubel edited and published *An American Primer* in 1904, it did not become well known until F.O. Matthiessen published *American Renaissance* in 1941. In that book, which initiated a lasting redefinition of the canon of American literature, Matthiessen's trailblazing reassessment of Whitman, as a "language experimenter," was based on the insights he derived from the *Primer*.

The final, and least well known, of the prose texts in this volume, "Walt Whitman in Camden," is the most moving for me. Whitman published it, under the pseudonym "George Selwyn," in 1885, thirty years after first writing about himself in the third person in the 1855 reviews. He's still at it. But now with what sweetness! with what poignant calm! with what achieved sanity! Still a rough, a boho, still a saunterer, a loiterer, taking his cane, his knapsack (you can see it there yet), hobbling down to the ferry, crossing the Delaware to chat with black folks and white folks, high and low, male and female, on Market Street, on Chestnut Street. In the evening he ferries home, thinking often of that other ferry, the Brooklyn Ferry he rode as boy and young man so many times, thinking of that other estuary. "Flow on river! flow with the flood-tide, and ebb with the ebb-tide!" He returns to his Camden "shanty," to his rude, simple, free-and-easy, old sailor's room, lights the good gas lamp, settles in his great cane-seat chair.

> Through his paralysis, poverty...incredible slanders...and the quite complete failure of his book from a worldly and financial point of view...amid bodily helplessness and a most meagre income, more vigorous and radiant than ever.

Oh yes, he is. And every atom belonging to him as good belongs to us. "I am with you, you men and women of a generation, or ever so many generations hence." And so he is, in the living text, which we herein strive to preserve.

# Old Age Echoes

## An Executor's Diary Note, 1891

I said to W. W. today: "Though you have put the finishing touches on the *Leaves*, closed them with your good-by, you will go on living a year or two longer and writing more poems. The question is, what will you do with these poems when the time comes to fix their place in the volume?"

"Do with them? I am not unprepared—I have even contemplated that emergency—I have a title in reserve: Old Age Echoes—applying not so much to things as to echoes of things, reverberant, an aftermath."

"You have dropt enough by the roadside, as you went along, from different editions, to make a volume. Some day the world will demand to have that put together somewhere."

"Do you think it?"

"Certainly. Should you put it under ban?"

"Why should I—how could I? So far as you may have anything to do with it I place upon you the injunction that whatever may be added to the *Leaves* shall be supplementary, avowed as such, leaving the book complete as I left it, consecutive to the point I left off, marking always an unmistakable, deep down, unobliterable division line. In the long run the world will do as it

45

pleases with the book. I am determined to have the world know what I was pleased to do."

Here is a late personal note from W. W.: "My tho't is to collect a lot of prose and poetry pieces—small or smallish mostly, but a few larger—appealing to the good will, the heart—sorrowful ones not rejected—but no morbid ones given."

There is no reason for doubt that "A Thought of Columbus," closing "Old Age Echoes," was W. W.'s last deliberate composition, dating December, 1891.

(Horace Traubel)

## To Soar in Freedom and in Fullness of Power

I have not so much emulated the birds that musically
     sing,
I have abandon'd myself to flights, broad circles.
The hawk, the seagull, have far more possess'd me than
     the canary or mocking-bird,
I have not felt to warble and trill, however sweetly,
I have felt to soar in freedom and in the fullness of
     power, joy, volition.

## Then Shall Perceive

In softness, languor, bloom, and growth,
Thine eyes, ears, all thy sense—thy loftiest attribute—
     all that takes cognizance of beauty,
Shall rouse and fill—then shall perceive!

## The Few Drops Known

Of heroes, history, grand events, premises, myths,
     poems,
The few drops known must stand for oceans of the
     unknown,
On this beautiful and thick peopl'd earth, here and there
     a little specimen put on record,

A little of Greeks and Romans, a few Hebrew canticles,
    a few death odors as from graves, from Egypt—
What are they to the long and copious retrospect of
    antiquity?


## One Thought Ever at the Fore

One thought ever at the fore—
That in the Divine Ship, the World, breasting Time and
    Space,
All Peoples of the globe together sail, sail the same
    voyage, are bound to the same destination.


## While Behind All Firm and Erect

While behind all, firm and erect as ever,
Undismay'd amid the rapids—amid the irresistible and
    deadly urge,
Stands a helmsman, with brow elate and strong hand.


## A Kiss to the Bride
**MARRIAGE OF NELLY GRANT, MAY 21, 1874**

Sacred, blithesome, undenied,
With benisons from East and West,
And salutations North and South,

Through me indeed to-day a million hearts and hands,
Wafting a million loves, a million soul felt prayers;

—Tender and true remain the arm that shields thee!
Fair winds always fill the ship's sails that sail thee!
Clear sun by day, and light stars at night, beam on thee!
Dear girl—through me the ancient privilege too,
For the New World, through me, the old, old wedding
    greeting:
O youth and health! O sweet Missouri rose! O bonny
    bride!
Yield thy red cheeks, thy lips, to-day,
Unto a Nation's loving kiss.


## *Nay, Tell Me Not To-day the Publish'd Shame*
WINTER OF 1873, CONGRESS IN SESSION

Nay, tell me not to-day the publish'd shame,
Read not to-day the journal's crowded page,
The merciless reports still branding forehead after
    forehead,
The guilty column following guilty column.

To-day to me the tale refusing,
Turning from it—from the white capitol turning,
Far from these swelling domes, topt with statues,
More endless, jubilant, vital visions rise
Unpublish'd, unreported.

Through all your quiet ways, or North or South, you
    Equal States, you honest farms,
Your million untold manly healthy lives, or East or
    West, city or country,
Your noiseless mothers, sisters, wives, unconscious of
    their good,
Your mass of homes nor poor nor rich, in visions rise—
    (even your excellent poverties,)
Your self-distilling, never-ceasing virtues, self-denials,
    graces,
Your endless base of deep integrities within, timid but
    certain,
Your blessings steadily bestow'd, sure as the light, and
    still,
(Plunging to these as a determin'd diver down the deep
    hidden waters,)
These, these to-day I brood upon—all else refusing,
    these will I con,
To-day to these give audience.


## Supplement Hours

Sane, random, negligent hours,
Sane, easy, culminating hours,
After the flush, the Indian summer, of my life,
Away from Books—away from Art—the lesson learn'd,
    pass'd o'er,
Soothing, bathing, merging all—the sane, magnetic,
Now for the day and night themselves—the open air,

Now for the fields, the seasons, insects, trees—the rain
    and snow,
Where wild bees flitting hum,
Or August mulleins grow, or winter's snowflakes fall,
Or stars in the skies roll round—
The silent sun and stars.

## Of Many a Smutch'd Deed Reminiscent

Full of wickedness, I—of many a smutch'd deed
    reminiscent—of worse deeds capable,
Yet I look composedly upon nature, drink day and night
    the joys of life, and await death with perfect
    equanimity,
Because of my tender and boundless love for him I love
    and because of his boundless love for me.

## To Be at All
CF. STANZA 27, "SONG OF MYSELF"

To be at all—what is better than that?
I think if there were nothing more developed, the clam
    in its callous shell in the sand were august enough.
I am not in any callous shell;
I am cased with supple conductors, all over,
They take every object by the hand, and lead it within
    me;
They are thousands, each one with his entry to himself;

They are always watching with their little eyes, from my
    head to my feet;
One no more than a point lets in and out of me such
    bliss and magnitude,
I think I could lift the girder of the house away if it lay
    between me and whatever I wanted.

## Death's Valley

TO ACCOMPANY A PICTURE; BY REQUEST.
"THE VALLEY OF THE SHADOW OF DEATH,"
FROM THE PAINTING BY GEORGE INNESS.

Nay, do not dream, designer dark,
Thou hast portray'd or hit thy theme entire;
I, hoverer of late by this dark valley, by its confines,
    having glimpses of it,
Here enter lists with thee, claiming my right to make a
    symbol too.
For I have seen many wounded soldiers die,
After dread suffering—have seen their lives pass off with
    smiles;
And I have watch'd the death-hours of the old; and seen
    the infant die;
The rich, with all his nurses and his doctors;
And then the poor, in meagerness and poverty;
And I myself for long, O Death, have breath'd my every
    breath
Amid the nearness and the silent thought of thee.
And out of these and thee,

I make a scene, a song (not fear of thee,
Nor gloom's ravines, nor bleak, nor dark—for I do not
  fear thee,
Nor celebrate the struggle, or contortion, or hard-tied
  knot),
Of the broad blessed light and perfect air, with
  meadows, rippling tides, and trees and flowers and
  grass,
And the low hum of living breeze—and in the midst
  God's beautiful eternal right hand,
Thee, holiest minister of Heaven—thee, envoy, usherer,
  guide at last of all,
Rich, florid, loosener of the stricture-knot call'd life,
Sweet, peaceful, welcome Death.


## On the Same Picture
### INTENDED FOR FIRST STANZA OF "DEATH'S VALLEY"

Aye, well I know 'tis ghastly to descend that valley:
Preachers, musicians, poets, painters, always render it,
Philosophs exploit—the battlefield, the ship at sea, the
  myriad beds, all lands,
All, all the past have enter'd, the ancientest humanity we
  know,
Syria's, India's, Egypt's, Greece's, Rome's;
Till now for us under our very eyes spreading the same
  to-day,

Grim, ready, the same to-day, for entrance, yours and
    mine,
Here, here 'tis limn'd.


## A Thought of Columbus

The mystery of mysteries, the crude and hurried
    ceaseless flame, spontaneous, bearing on itself.
The bubble and the huge, round, concrete orb!
A breath of Deity, as thence the bulging universe
    unfolding!
The many issuing cycles from their precedent minute!
The eras of the soul incepting in an hour,
Haply the widest, farthest evolutions of the world and
    man.


Thousands and thousands of miles hence, and now four
    centuries back,
A mortal impulse thrilling its brain cell,
Reck'd or unreck'd, the birth can no longer be
    postpon'd:
A phantom of the moment, mystic, stalking, sudden,
Only a silent thought, yet toppling down of more than
    walls of brass or stone.
(A flutter at the darkness' edge as if old Time's and
    Space's secret near revealing.)
A thought! a definite thought works out in shape.
Four hundred years roll on.

The rapid cumulus—trade, navigation, war, peace,
democracy, roll on;
The restless armies and the fleets of time following their
leader—the old camps of ages pitch'd in newer,
larger areas,
The tangl'd, long-deferr'd eclaircissement of human life
and hopes boldly begins untying,
As here to-day up-grows the Western World.

(An added word yet to my song, far Discoverer, as ne'er
before sent back to son of earth—
If still thou hearest, hear me,
Voicing as now—lands, races, arts, bravas to thee,
O'er the long backward path to thee—one vast
consensus, north, south, east, west,
Soul plaudits! acclamation! reverent echoes!
One manifold, huge memory to thee! oceans and lands!
The modern world to thee and thought of thee!)

# Fallen Leaves I

POEMS DROPPED FROM
*LEAVES OF GRASS*

*Respondez! (Poem of the Propositions of Nakedness)*

RESPONDEZ! Respondez!
(The war is completed—the price is paid—the title is
    settled beyond recall;)
Let every one answer! let those who sleep be waked! let
    none evade!
Must we still go on with our affectations and sneaking?
Let me bring this to a close—I pronounce openly for a
    new distribution of roles;
Let that which stood in front go behind! and let that
    which was behind advance to the front and speak;
Let murderers, bigots, fools, unclean persons, offer new
    propositions!
Let the old propositions be postponed!
Let faces and theories be turn'd inside out! let meanings
    be freely criminal, as well as results!
Let there be no suggestion above the suggestion of
    drudgery!
Let none be pointed toward his destination! (Say! do
    you know your destination?)
Let men and women be mock'd with bodies and mock'd
    with Souls!
Let the love that waits in them, wait! let it die, or pass
    still-born to other spheres!

59

Let the sympathy that waits in every man, wait! or let it
   also pass, a dwarf, to other spheres!
Let contradictions prevail! let one thing contradict
   another! and let one line of my poems contradict
   another!
Let the people sprawl with yearning, aimless hands!
   let their tongues be broken! let their eyes be
   discouraged! let none descend into their hearts
   with the fresh lusciousness of love!
(Stifled, O days! O lands! in every public and private
   corruption!
Smother'd in thievery, impotence, shamelessness,
   mountain-high;
Brazen effrontery, scheming, rolling like ocean's waves
   around and upon you, O my days! my lands!
For not even those thunderstorms, nor fiercest lightnings
   of the war, have purified the atmosphere;)
—Let the theory of America still be management, caste,
   comparison!
   (Say! what other theory would you?)
Let them that distrust birth and death still lead the rest!
   (Say! why shall they not lead you?)
Let the crust of hell be neared and trod on! let the days
   be darker than the nights! let slumber bring less
   slumber than waking time brings!
Let the world never appear to him or her for whom it
   was all made!
Let the heart of the young man still exile itself from the
   heart of the old man! and let the heart of the old
   man be exiled from that of the young man!

Let the sun and moon go! let scenery take the applause
of the audience! let there be apathy under the stars!
Let freedom prove no man's inalienable right! every one
who can tyrannize, let him tyrannize to his satisfac-
tion!
Let none but infidels be countenanced!
Let the eminence of meanness, treachery, sarcasm, hate,
greed, indecency, impotence, lust, be taken for
granted above all! let writers, judges, governments,
households, religions, philosophies, take such for
granted above all!
Let the worst men beget children out of the worst
women!
Let the priest still play at immortality!
Let death be inaugurated!
Let nothing remain but the ashes of teachers, artists,
moralists, lawyers, and learn'd and polite persons!
Let him who is without my poems be assassinated!
Let the cow, the horse, the camel, the garden-bee—let
the mud-fish, the lobster, the mussel, eel, the sting-
ray, and the grunting pig-fish—let these, and the
like of these, be put on a perfect equality with man
and woman!
Let churches accommodate serpents, vermin, and the
corpses of those who have died of the most filthy of
diseases!
Let marriage slip down among fools, and be for none
but fools!
Let men among themselves talk and think forever
obscenely of women! and let women among
themselves talk and think obscenely of men!

Let us all, without missing one, be exposed in public,
    naked, monthly, at the peril of our lives! let our
    bodies be freely handled and examined by whoever
    chooses!
Let nothing but copies at second hand be permitted to
    exist upon the earth!
Let the earth desert God, nor let there ever henceforth
    be mention'd the name of God!
Let there be no God!
Let there be money, business, imports, exports, custom,
    authority, precedents, pallor, dyspepsia, smut,
    ignorance, unbelief!
Let judges and criminals be transposed! let the prison-
    keepers be put in prison! let those that were
    prisoners take the keys! (Say! why might they not
    just as well be transposed?)
Let the slaves be masters! let the masters become slaves!
Let the reformers descend from the stands where they
    are forever bawling! let an idiot or insane person
    appear on each of the stands!
Let the Asiatic, the African, the European, the
    American, and the Australian, go armed against the
    murderous stealthiness of each other! let them
    sleep armed! let none believe in good will!
Let there be no unfashionable wisdom! let such be
    scorn'd and derided off from the earth!
Let a floating cloud in the sky—let a wave of the sea—
    let growing mint, spinach, onions, tomatoes—let
    these be exhibited as shows, at a great price for
    admission!

Let all the men of These States stand aside for a few
    smouchers! let the few seize on what they choose!
    let the rest gawk, giggle, starve, obey!
Let shadows be furnish'd with genitals! let substances be
    deprived of their genitals!
Let there be wealthy and immense cities—but still
    through any of them, not a single poet, savior,
    knower, lover!
Let the infidels of These States laugh all faith away!
If one man be found who has faith, let the rest set upon
    him!
Let them affright faith! let them destroy the power of
    breeding faith!
Let the she-harlots and the he-harlots be prudent!
    let them dance on, while seeming lasts!
    (O seeming! seeming! seeming!)
Let the preachers recite creeds! let them still teach only
    what they have been taught!
Let insanity still have charge of sanity!
Let books take the place of trees, animals, rivers, clouds!
Let the daub'd portraits of heroes supersede heroes!
Let the manhood of man never take steps after itself!
Let it take steps after eunuchs, and after consumptive
    and genteel persons!
Let the white person again tread the black person under
    his heel! (Say! which is trodden under heel, after
    all?)
Let the reflections of the things of the world be studied
    in mirrors! let the things themselves still continue
    unstudied!

Let a man seek pleasure everywhere except in himself!
Let a woman seek happiness everywhere except in
　　herself!
(What real happiness have you had one single hour
　　through your whole life?)
Let the limited years of life do nothing for the limitless
　　years of death! (What do you suppose death will
　　do, then?)


## Poem of Remembrances
## for a Girl or a Boy of These States*

You just maturing youth! You male or female!
Remember the organic compact of These States,
Remember the pledge of the Old Thirteen
　　thenceforward to the rights, life, liberty, equality
　　of man,
Remember what was promulged by the founders,
　　ratified by The States, signed in black and white by
　　the Commissioners, and read by Washington at the
　　head of the army,
Remember the purposes of the founders,—Remember
　　Washington;
Remember the copious humanity streaming from every
　　direction toward America;

---

*In the 1867 *Leaves*, Whitman printed the last nine stanzas of "Poem of
Remembrances for a Girl or a Boy of These States" as a complete poem
under the title "Think of the Soul," and discarded the rest.

Remember the hospitality that belongs to nations and
    men; (Cursed be nation, woman, man, without
    hospitality!)
Remember, government is to subserve individuals,
Not any, not the President, is to have one jot more than
    you or me,
Not any habitan of America is to have one jot less than
    you or me.

Anticipate when the thirty or fifty millions, are to
    become the hundred, or two hundred millions, of
    equal freemen and freewomen, amicably joined.

Recall ages—One age is but a part—ages are but a part;
Recall the angers, bickerings, delusions, superstitions, of
    the idea of caste,
Recall the bloody cruelties and crimes.

Anticipate the best women;
I say an unnumbered new race of hardy and well-
    defined women are to spread through all These
    States,
I say a girl fit for These States must be free, capable,
    dauntless, just the same as a boy.

Anticipate your own life—retract with merciless power,
Shirk nothing—retract in time—Do you see those
    errors, diseases, weaknesses, lies, thefts?

Do you see that lost character—Do you see decay,
  consumption, rum-drinking, dropsy, fever, mortal
  cancer or inflammation?
Do you see death, and the approach of death?

Think of the Soul;
I swear to you that body of yours gives proportions to
  your Soul somehow to live in other spheres;
I do not know how, but I know it is so.

Think of loving and being loved;
I swear to you, whoever you are, you can interfuse
  yourself with such things that everybody that sees
  you shall look longingly upon you.

Think of the past;
I warn you that in a little while others will find their
  past in you and your times.

The race is never separated—nor man nor woman
  escapes;
All is inextricable—things, spirits, Nature, nations, you
  too—from precedents you come.

Recall the ever—welcome defiers, (The mothers
  precede them;)
Recall the sages, poets, saviors, inventors, lawgivers, of
  the earth;

Recall Christ, brother of rejected persons—brother of
    slaves, felons, idiots, and of insane and diseas'd
    persons.

Think of the time when you were not yet born;
Think of times you stood at the side of the dying;
Think of the time when your own body will be dying.

Think of spiritual results,
Sure as the earth swims through the heavens, does every
    one of its objects pass into spiritual results.

Think of manhood, and you to be a man;
Do you count manhood, and the sweet of manhood,
    nothing?

Think of womanhood, and you to be a woman;
The creation is womanhood;
Have I not said that womanhood involves all?
Have I not told how the universe has nothing better
    than the best womanhood?


## *Enfans d' Adam*

In the new garden, in all the parts,
In cities now, modern, I wander,
Through the second or third result, or still further,
    primitive yet,
Days, places, indifferent—though various, the same,

Time, Paradise, the Mannahatta, the prairies, finding
    me unchanged,
Death indifferent—Is it that I lived long since?
    Was I buried very long ago?
For all that, I may now be watching you here, this
    moment;
For the future, with determined will, I seek—the
    woman of the future,
You, born years, centuries after me, I seek.

## Calamus 5*

States!
Were you looking to be held together by the lawyers?
By an agreement on a paper? Or by arms?

Away!
I arrive, bringing these, beyond all the forces of courts
    and arms,
These! to hold you together as firmly as the earth itself
    is held together.

The old breath of life, ever new,
Here! I pass it by contract to you, America.

O mother! have you done much for me?
Behold, there shall from me be much done for you.

---

*Whitman recycled lines from this poem into "Over the Carnage Rose
Phophetic a Voice" and "For You O Democracy."

There shall from me be a new friendship—It shall be
    called after my name,
It shall circulate through The States, indifferent of
    place,
It shall twist and intertwist them through and around
    each other—Compact shall they be, showing new
    signs,
Affection shall solve every one of the problems of
    freedom,
Those who love each other shall be invincible,
They shall finally make America completely victorious,
    in my name.
One from Massachusetts shall be a comrade to a
    Missourian,
One from Maine or Vermont, and a Carolinian and an
    Oregonese, shall be friends triune, more precious
    to each other than all the riches of the earth.

To Michigan shall be wafted perfume from Florida,
To the Mannahatta from Cuba or Mexico,
Not the perfume of flowers, but sweeter, and wafted
    beyond death.

No danger shall balk Columbia's lovers,
If need be, a thousand shall sternly immolate themselves
    for one,
The Kanuck shall be willing to lay down his life for the
    Kansian, and the Kansian for the Kanuck, on due
    need.

It shall be customary in all directions, in the houses and
    streets, to see manly affection,
The departing brother or friend shall salute the
    remaining brother or friend with a kiss.

There shall be innovations,
There shall be countless linked hands—namely, the
    Northeasterner's and the Northwesterner's, and the
    Southwesterner's, and those of the interior, and all
    their brood,
These shall be masters of the world under a new power,
They shall laugh to scorn the attacks of all the
    remainder of the world.

The most dauntless and rude shall touch face to face
    lightly,
The dependence of Liberty shall be lovers,
The continuance of Equality shall be comrades.

These shall tie and band stronger than hoops of iron,
I, extatic, O partners! O lands! henceforth with the love
    of lovers tie you.

I will make the continent indissoluble,
I will make the most splendid race the sun ever yet
    shone upon,
I will make divine magnetic lands.

I will plant companionship thick as trees along all the
    rivers of America, and along the shores of the great
    lakes, and all over the prairies,

I will make inseparable cities, with their arms about
    each other's necks.

For you these, from me, O Democracy, to serve you, ma
    femme!
For you! for you, I am trilling these songs.


## *Calamus 8*

Long I thought that knowledge alone would suffice
    me—O if I could but obtain knowledge!
Then my lands engrossed me—Lands of the prairies,
    Ohio's land, the southern savannas, engrossed
    me—For them I would live—I would be their
    orator;
Then I met the examples of old and new heroes—I
    heard of warriors, sailors, and all dauntless
    persons—And it seemed to me that I too had it in
    me to be as dauntless as any—and would be so;
And then, to enclose all, it came to me to strike up the
    songs of the New World—And then I believed my
    life must be spent in singing;
But now take notice, land of the prairies, land of the
    south savannas, Ohio's land,
Take notice, you Kanuck woods—and you Lake
    Huron—and all that with you roll toward
    Niagara—and you Niagara also,
And you, Californian mountains—That you each and all
    find somebody else to be your singer of songs,

For I can be your singer of songs no longer—One who
    loves me is jealous of me, and withdraws me from
    all but love,
With the rest I dispense—I sever from what I thought
    would suffice me, for it does not—it is now empty
    and tasteless to me,
I heed knowledge, and the grandeur of The States, and
    the examples of heroes, no more,
I am indifferent to my own songs—I will go with him I
    love,
It is to be enough for us that we are together—We
    never separate again.

## Calamus 9

Hours continuing long, sore and heavy-hearted,
Hours of the dusk, when I withdraw to a lonesome and
    unfrequented spot, seating myself, leaning my face
    in my hands;
Hours sleepless, deep in the night, when I go forth,
    speeding swiftly the country roads, or through the
    city streets, or pacing miles and miles, stifling
    plaintive cries;
Hours discouraged, distracted—for the one I cannot
    content myself without, soon I saw him content
    himself without me;

Hours when I am forgotten, (O weeks and months are
    passing, but I believe I am never to forget!)
Sullen and suffering hours! (I am ashamed—but it is
    useless—I am what I am;)
Hours of my torment—I wonder if other men ever have
    the like, out of the like feelings?
Is there even one other like me—distracted—his friend,
    his lover, lost to him?
Is he too as I am now? Does he still rise in the morning,
    dejected, thinking who is lost to him? and at night,
    awaking, think who is lost?
Does he too harbor his friendship silent and endless?
    harbor his anguish and passion?
Does some stray reminder, or the casual mention of a
    name, bring the fit back upon him, taciturn and
    deprest?
Does he see himself reflected in me? In these hours,
    does he see the face of his hours reflected?

## Calamus 16

Who is now reading this?

May-be one is now reading this who knows some
    wrong-doing of my past life,
Or may-be a stranger is reading this who has secretly
    loved me,

Or may-be one who meets all my grand assumptions
    and egotisms with derision,
Or may-be one who is puzzled at me.

As if I were not puzzled at myself!
Or as if I never deride myself! (O conscience-struck! O
    self-convicted!)
Or as if I do not secretly love strangers! (O tenderly, a
    long time, and never avow it;)
Or as if I did not see, perfectly well, interior in myself,
    the stuff of wrong-doing,
Or as if it could cease transpiring from me until it must
    cease.


## *Thoughts 1*

Of the visages of things—And of piercing through to
    the accepted hells beneath;
Of ugliness—To me there is just as much in it as there is
    in beauty—And now the ugliness of human beings
    is acceptable to me;
Of detected persons—To me, detected persons are not,
    in any respect, worse than undetected persons—
    and are not in any respect worse than I am myself;
Of criminals—To me, any judge, or any juror, is equally
    criminal—and any reputable person is also—and
    the President is also.

## *Thoughts 2*

Of waters, forests, hills,
Of the earth at large, whispering through medium of
    me;
Of vista—Suppose some sight in arriere, through the
    formative chaos, presuming the growth, fulness,
    life, now attained on the journey;
(But I see the road continued, and the journey ever
    continued;)
Of what was once lacking on the earth, and in due time
    has become supplied—And of what will yet be
    supplied,
Because all I see and know, I believe to have purport in
    what will yet be supplied.

## *Thoughts 4*

Of ownership—As if one fit to own things could not at
    pleasure enter upon all, and incorporate them into
    himself or herself;
Of Equality—As if it harmed me, giving others the same
    chances and rights as myself—As if it were not
    indispensable to my own rights that others possess
    the same;

Of Justice—As if Justice could be any thing but the
    same ample law, expounded by natural judges and
    saviours,
As if it might be this thing or that thing, according to
    decisions.


## Thoughts 6

Of what I write from myself—As if that were not the
    resumé;
Of Histories—As if such, however complete, were not
    less complete than my poems;
As if the shreds, the records of nations, could possibly
    be as lasting as my poems;
As if here were not the amount of all nations, and of all
    the lives of heroes.


## So far, and so far, and on toward the end

So far, and so far, and on toward the end,
Singing what is sung in this book, from the irresistible
    impulses of me;
But whether I continue beyond this book, to maturity,
Whether I shall dart forth the true rays, the ones that
    wait unfired,
(Did you think the sun was shining its brightest?
No—it has not yet fully risen;)

Whether I shall complete what is here started,
Whether I shall attain my own height, to justify these,
	yet unfinished,
Whether I shall make THE POEM OF THE NEW WORLD,
	transcending all others—depends, rich persons,
	upon you,
Depends, whoever you are now filling the current
	Presidentiad, upon you,
Upon you, Governor, Mayor, Congressman,
And you, contemporary America.


## Says


### 1
I say whatever tastes sweet to the most perfect person,
	that is finally right.


### 2
I say nourish a great intellect, a great brain;
If I have said anything to the contrary, I hereby retract
	it.


### 3
I say man shall not hold property in man;
I say the least developed person on earth is just as
	important and sacred to himself or herself, as the
	most developed person is to himself or herself.

4

I say where liberty draws not the blood out of slavery,
    there slavery draws the blood out of liberty,
I say the word of the good old cause in These States,
    and resound it hence over the world.


5

I say the human shape or face is so great, it must never
    be made ridiculous;
I say for ornaments nothing outre can be allowed,
And that anything is most beautiful without ornament,
And that exaggerations will be sternly revenged in your
    own physiology, and in other persons' physiology
    also;
And I say that clean—shaped children can be jetted and
    conceived only where natural forms prevail in
    public, and the human face and form are never
    caricatured;
And I say that genius need never more be turned to
    romances,
(For facts properly told, how mean appear all
    romances.)


6

I say the word of lands fearing nothing—I will have no
    other land;
I say discuss all and expose all—I am for every topic
    openly;

I say there can be no salvation for These States without
    innovators—without free tongues, and ears willing
    to hear the tongues;
And I announce as a glory of These States, that they
    respectfully listen to propositions, reforms, fresh
    views and doctrines, from successions of men and
    women,
Each age with its own growth.

### 7

I have said many times that materials and the Soul are
    great, and that all depends on physique;
Now I reverse what I said, and affirm that all depends
    on the aesthetic or intellectual,
And that criticism is great—and that refinement is
    greatest of all;
And I affirm now that the mind governs—and that all
    depends on the mind.

### 8

With one man or woman—(no matter which one—I
    even pick out the lowest,)
With him or her I now illustrate the whole law;
I say that every right, in politics or what-not, shall be
    eligible to that one man or woman, on the same
    terms as any.

## Apostroph*

O mater! O fils!
O brood continental!
O flowers of the prairies!
O space boundless! O hum of mighty products!
O you teeming cities! O so invincible, turbulent, proud!
O race of the future! O women!
O fathers! O you men of passion and the storm!
O native power only! O beauty!
O yourself! O God! O divine average!
O you bearded roughs! O bards! O all those slumberers!
O arouse! the dawn-bird's throat sounds shrill! Do you
    not hear the cock crowing?
O, as I walk'd the beach, I heard the mournful notes
    foreboding a tempest—the low, oft-repeated shriek
    of the diver, the long-lived loon;
O I heard, and yet hear, angry thunder;—O you sailors!
    O ships! make quick preparation!
O from his masterful sweep, the warning cry of the
    eagle!
(Give way there, all! It is useless! Give up your spoils;)
O sarcasms! Propositions! (O if the whole world should
    prove indeed a sham, a sell!)

---

*This and the following poem neatly illustrate Whitman's constant revision. "Apostroph" first appeared in the 1860 *Leaves*. In 1867 he replaced it with "O Sun of Real Peace," which is a rewrite of the last 19 lines of "Apostroph." In 1867, he dropped "O Sun of Real Peace" as well.

O I believe there is nothing real but America and
    freedom!
O to sternly reject all except Democracy!
O imperator! O who dare confront you and me?
O to promulgate our own! O to build for that which
    builds for mankind!
O feuillage! O North! O the slope drained by the
    Mexican sea!
O all, all inseparable—ages, ages, ages!
O a curse on him that would dissever this Union for any
    reason whatever!
O climates, labors! O good and evil! O death!
O you strong with iron and wood! O Personality!
O the village or place which has the greatest man or
    woman! even if it be only a few ragged huts;
O the city where women walk in public processions in
    the streets, the same as the men;
O a wan and terrible emblem, by me adopted!
O shapes arising! shapes of the future centuries!
O muscle and pluck forever for me!
O workmen and workwomen forever for me!
O farmers and sailors! O drivers of horses forever for
    me!
O I will make the new bardic list of trades and tools!
O you coarse and wilful! I love you!
O South! O longings for my dear home! O soft and
    sunny airs!
O pensive! O I must return where the palm grows and
    the mocking-bird sings, or else I die!

O equality! O organic compacts! I am come to be your
    born poet!
O whirl, contest, sounding and resounding! I am your
    poet, because I am part of you;
O days by-gone! Enthusiasts! Antecedents!
O vast preparations for These States! O years!
O what is now being sent forward thousands of years to
    come!
O mediums! O to teach! to convey the invisible faith!
To promulge real things! to journey through all The
    States!
O creation! O to-day! O laws! O unmitigated adoration!
O for mightier broods of orators, artists, and singers!
O for native songs! carpenter's, boatman's, ploughman's
    songs! shoemaker's songs!
O haughtiest growth of time! O free and extatic!
O what I, here, preparing, warble for!
O you hastening light! O the sun of the world will
    ascend, dazzling, and take his height—and you too
    will ascend;
O so amazing and so broad! up there resplendent,
    darting and burning;
O prophetic! O vision staggered with weight of light!
    with pouring glories!
O copious! O hitherto unequalled!
O Libertad! O compact! O union impossible to
    dissever!
O my Soul! O lips becoming tremulous, powerless!
O centuries, centuries yet ahead!
O voices of greater orators! I pause—I listen for you!

O you States, Cities! defiant of all outside authority! I
    spring at once into your arms! you I most love!
O you grand Presidentiads! I wait for you!
New history! New heroes! I project you!
Visions of poets! only you really last! O sweep on! sweep
    on!
O Death! O you striding there! O I cannot yet!
O heights! O infinitely too swift and dizzy yet!
O purged lumine! you threaten me more than I can
    stand!
O present! I return while yet I may to you!
O poets to come, I depend upon you!

## O Sun of Real Peace

O sun of real peace! O hastening light!
O free and extatic! O what I here, preparing, warble for!
O the sun of the world will ascend, dazzling, and take
    his height—and you too, O my Ideal, will surely
    ascend!
O so amazing and broad—and up there resplendent,
    darting and burning!
O vision prophetic, stagger'd with weight of light! with
    pouring glories!
O lips of my soul, already becoming powerless!
O ample and grand Presidentiads! Now the war, the war
    is over!
New history! new heroes! I project you!
Visions of poets! only you really last! sweep on! sweep
    on!

O heights too swift and dizzy yet!
O purged and luminous! you threaten me more than I
    can stand!
(I must not venture—the ground under my feet menaces
    me—it will not support me:
O future too immense,)—O present, I return, while yet
    I may, to you.


## To my Soul

1.    As nearing departure,
       As the time draws nigh, glooming from you,
       A cloud—a dread beyond, of I know not what,
          darkens me.

2.    I shall go forth,
       I shall traverse The States—but I cannot tell
          whither or how long;
       Perhaps soon, some day or night while I am
          singing, my voice will suddenly cease.

3.    O Soul!
       Then all may arrive to but this;
       The glances of my eyes, that swept the daylight,
       The unspeakable love I interchanged with women,
       My joys in the open air—my walks through the
          Mannahatta,

The continual good will I have met—the curious
    attachment of young men to me,
My reflections alone—the absorption into me from
    the landscape, stars, animals, thunder, rain,
    and snow, in my wanderings alone,
The words of my mouth, rude, ignorant,
    arrogant—my many faults and derelictions,
The light touches, on my lips, of the lips of my
    comrades, at parting,
The tracks which I leave, upon the side-walks and
    fields,
May but arrive at this beginning of me,
This beginning of me—and yet it is enough, O
    Soul,
O Soul, we have positively appeared—that is
enough.


## Now Lift Me Close

Now lift me close to your face till I whisper,
What you are holding is in reality no book, nor part of a
    book;
It is a man, flush'd and full-blooded—it is I—*So long!*
—We must separate awhile—Here! take from my lips
    this kiss;
Whoever you are, I give it especially to you;
*So long!*—And I hope we shall meet again.

## To the Reader at Parting

Now, dearest comrade, lift me to your face,
We must separate awhile—Here! take from my lips this
    kiss;
Whoever you are, I give it especially to you;
*So long!*—And I hope we shall meet again.


## To You

Let us twain walk aside from the rest;
Now we are together privately, do you discard
    ceremony;
Come! vouchsafe to me what has yet been vouchsafed to
    none—Tell me the whole story,
Let us talk of death—unbosom all freely,
Tell me what you would not tell your brother, wife,
    husband, or physician.


## Debris

He is wisest who has the most caution,
He only wins who goes far enough.

Any thing is as good as established, when that is
    established that will produce it and continue it.

What General has a good army in himself, has a good
    army;
He happy in himself, or she happy in herself, is happy,
But I tell you you cannot be happy by others, any more
    than you can beget or conceive a child by others.

Have you learned lessons only of those who admired
    you, and were tender with you, and stood aside for
    you?
Have you not learned the great lessons of those who
    rejected you, and braced themselves against you? or
    who treated you with contempt, or disputed the
    passage with you?
Have you had no practice to receive opponents when
    they come?

Despairing cries float ceaselessly toward me, day and
    night,
The sad voice of Death—the call of my nearest lover,
    putting forth, alarmed, uncertain,
*This sea I am quickly to sail, come tell me,*
*Come tell me where I am speeding—tell me my destination.*

I understand your anguish, but I cannot help you,
I approach, hear, behold—the sad mouth, the look out
    of the eyes, your mute inquiry,
*Whither I go from the bed I now recline on, come tell me;*
Old age, alarmed, uncertain—A young woman's voice
    appealing to me, for comfort,
A young man's voice, *Shall I not escape?*

A thousand perfect men and women appear,
Around each gathers a cluster of friends, and gay
    children and youths, with offerings.

A mask—a perpetual natural disguiser of herself,
Concealing her face, concealing her form,
Changes and transformations every hour, every
    movement,
Falling upon her even when she sleeps.

One sweeps by, attended by an immense train,
All emblematic of peace—not a soldier or menial among
    them.

One sweeps by, old, with black eyes, and profuse white
    hair,
He has the simple magnificence of health and strength,
His face strikes as with flashes of lightning whoever it
    turns toward.

Three old men slowly pass, followed by three others,
    and they by three others,
They are beautiful—the one in the middle of each
    group holds his companions by the hand,
As they walk, they give out perfume wherever they walk.

Women sit, or move to and fro—some old, some young,
The young are beautiful—but the old are more
    beautiful than the young.

What weeping face is that looking from the window?
Why does it stream those sorrowful tears?
Is it for some burial place, vast and dry?
Is it to wet the soil of graves?

I will take an egg out of the robin's nest in the orchard,
I will take a branch of gooseberries from the old bush in
    the garden, and go and preach to the world;
You shall see I will not meet a single heretic or scorner,
You shall see how I stump clergymen, and confound
    them,
You shall see me showing a scarlet tomato, and a white
    pebble from the beach.

Behavior—fresh, native, copious, each one for himself
    or herself,
Nature and the Soul expressed—America and freedom
    expressed—In it the finest art,
In it pride, cleanliness, sympathy, to have their chance,
In it physique, intellect, faith—in it just as much as to
    manage an army or a city, or to write a book—
    perhaps more,
The youth, the laboring person, the poor person,
    rivalling all the rest—perhaps outdoing the rest,
The effects of the universe no greater than its;
For there is nothing in the whole universe that can be
    more effective than a man's or woman's daily
    behavior can be,
In any position, in any one of These States.

Not the pilot has charged himself to bring his ship into
  port, though beaten back, and many times baffled,
Not the path-finder, penetrating inland, weary and
  long,
By deserts parched, snows chilled, rivers wet, perseveres
  till he reaches his destination,
More than I have charged myself, heeded or unheeded,
  to compose a free march for These States,
To be exhilarating music to them, years, centuries
  hence.

I thought I was not alone, walking here by the shore,
But the one I thought was with me, as now I walk by the
  shore,
As I lean and look through the glimmering light—that
  one has utterly disappeared,
And those appear that perplex me.


## Bathed in War's Perfume

Bathed in war's perfume—delicate flag!
(Should the days needing armies, needing fleets, come
  again,)
O to hear you call the sailors and the soldiers! flag like a
  beautiful woman!

O to hear the tramp, tramp, of a million answering
    men! O the ships they arm with joy!
O to see you leap and beckon from the tall masts of
    ships!
O to see you peering down on the sailors on the decks!
Flag like the eyes of women.


## Solid, Ironical, Rolling Orb

Solid, ironical, rolling orb!
Master of all, and matter of fact!—at last I accept your
    terms;
Bringing to practical, vulgar tests, of all my ideal
    dreams,
And of me, as lover and hero.


## Up, Lurid Stars!

Up, lurid stars! martial constellation!
Change, tattered cloth—your silver group withdrawing;
Bring we threads of scarlet, in vacant spots resetting,
    Thirty-four stars, red as blood.

World, take good notice! the silver group has vanished;
Notice clustering now, as coals of molten iron,
Time, warning baleful, off these western shores,
    Thirty-four stars, red as blood.

## Not My Enemies Ever Invade Me

Not my enemies ever invade me—no harm to my pride
    from them I fear;
But the lovers I recklessly love—lo! how they master
    me!
Lo! me, ever open and helpless, bereft of my strength!
Utterly abject, grovelling on the ground before them.

## This Day, O Soul

This day, O Soul, I give you a wondrous mirror;
Long in the dark, in tarnish and cloud it lay—But the
    cloud has pass'd, and the tarnish gone;
...Behold, O Soul! it is now a clean and bright mirror,
Faithfully showing you all the things of the world.

## When I Read the Book*

When I read the book, the biography famous;
And is this, then, (said I,) what the author calls a man's
    life?
And so will some one, when I am dead and gone, write
    my life?

---

*With its end interestingly rewritten, "When I Read the Book" appears in
the "Inscriptions" cluster of the deathbed *Leaves*.

(As if any man really knew aught of my life;
As if you, O cunning Soul, did not keep your secret
    well!)

## Lessons

There are who teach only the sweet lessons of peace and
    safety;
But I teach lessons of war and death to those I love,
That they readily meet invasions, when they come.

## Ashes of Soldiers: Epigraph

Again a verse for sake of you,
You soldiers in the ranks—you Volunteers,
Who bravely fighting, silent fell,
To fill unmention'd graves.

## One Song, America, Before I Go*

One song, America, before I go,
I'd sing, o'er all the rest, with trumpet sound,
For thee—the Future.

I'd sow a seed for thee of endless Nationality;

---

*Whitman worked lines 4-8 of "One Song, America, Before I Go" into the
first section of "Thou Mother with Thy Equal Brood."

I'd fashion thy Ensemble, including Body and Soul;
I'd show, away ahead, thy real Union, and how it may be
    accomplish'd.

(The paths to the House I seek to make,
But leave to those to come, the House itself.)


## Souvenirs of Democracy*

The business man, the acquirer vast,
After assiduous years, surveying results, preparing for
    departure,
Devises houses and lands to his children—bequeaths
    stocks, goods—funds for a school or hospital,
Leaves money to certain companions to buy tokens,
    souvenirs of gems and gold;
Parceling out with care—And then, to prevent all cavil,
His name to his testament formally signs.

But I, my life surveying,
With nothing to show, to devise, from its idle years,
Nor houses, nor lands—nor tokens of gems or gold for
    my friends,
Only these Souvenirs of Democracy—In them—in all
    my songs—behind me leaving,

---

*With revisions and cuts, "Souvenirs of Democracy" became the 1881
poem "My Legacy."

To You, whoever you are, (bathing, leavening this leaf
    especially with my breath—pressing on it a
    moment with my own hands;
—Here! feel how the pulse beats in my wrists!—
    how my heart's-blood is swelling, contracting!)
I will You, in all, Myself, with promise to never desert
    you,
To which I sign my name,

*Walt Whitman*

## From My Last Years

From my last years, last thoughts I here bequeath,
Scatter'd and dropt, in seeds, and wafted to the West,
Through moisture of Ohio, prairie soil of Illinois—
    through Colorado, California air,
For Time to germinate fully.

## In Former Songs

In former songs Pride have I sung, and Love, and
    passionate, joyful Life,
But here I twine the strands of Patriotism and Death.

And now, Life, Pride, Love, Patriotism and Death,
To you, O FREEDOM, purport of all!
(You that elude me most—refusing to be caught in
     songs of mine,)
I offer all to you.

### 2

'Tis not for nothing, Death,
I sound out you, and words of you, with daring tone—
     embodying you,
In my new Democratic chants—keeping you for a close,
For last impregnable retreat—a citadel and tower,
For my last stand—my pealing, final cry.

## Two Rivulets

Two Rivulets side by side,
Two blended, parallel, strolling tides,
Companions, travelers, gossiping as they journey.
For the Eternal Ocean bound,
These ripples, passing surges, streams of Death and
     Life,
Object and Subject hurrying, whirling by,
The Real and Ideal,

Alternate ebb and flow the Days and Nights,
(Strands of a Trio twining, Present, Future, Past.)

In You, whoe'er you are, my book perusing,
In I myself—in all the World—these ripples flow,
All, all, toward the mystic Ocean tending.

(O yearnful waves! the kisses of your lips!
Your breast so broad, with open arms, O firm, expanded
    shore!)


## *After an Interval*
### (NOV. 22, 1875, MIDNIGHT—
### SATURN AND MARS IN CONJUNCTION)

After an interval, reading, here in the midnight,
With the great stars looking on—all the stars of Orion
    looking,
And the silent Pleiades—and the duo looking of Saturn
    and ruddy Mars;
Pondering, reading my own songs, after a long interval,
    (sorrow and death familiar now,)
Ere closing the book, what pride! what joy! to find
    them,
Standing so well the test of death and night!
And the duo of Saturn and Mars!

## Or from That Sea of Time*

1

Or, from that Sea of Time,
Spray, blown by the wind—a double winrow-drift of
    weeds and shells;
(O little shells, so curious-convolute! so limpid-cold and
    voiceless!
Yet will you not, to the tympans of temples held,
Murmurs and echoes still bring up—Eternity's music,
    faint and far,
Wafted inland, sent from Atlantica's rim—strains for the
    Soul of the Prairies,

Whisper'd reverberations—chords for the ear of the
    West, joyously sounding
Your tidings old, yet ever new and untranslatable;)
Infinitesimals out of my life, and many a life,
(For not my life and years alone I give—all, all I give;)
These thoughts and Songs—waifs from the deep—here,
    cast high and dry,
Wash'd on America's shores.

2

Currents of starting a Continent new,
Overtures sent to the solid out of the liquid,

---

*Lines from "Or from That Sea of Time" and from "Two Rivulets" were
recycled into "As Consequent, Etc..."

Fusion of ocean and land—tender and pensive waves,
(Not safe and peaceful only—waves rous'd and ominous
    too,
Out of the depths, the storm's abysms—Who knows
    whence? Death's waves,
Raging over the vast, with many a broken spar and
    tatter'd sail.)


## [Last Droplets]

Last droplets of and after spontaneous rain,
From many limpid distillations and past showers;
(Will they germinate anything? mere exhalations as they
    all are—the land's and sea's—America's;
Will they filter to any deep emotion? any heart and
    brain?)


## After the Argument

A group of little children with their ways and chatter
    flow in,
Like welcome, rippling water o'er my heated nerves and
    flesh.

# Fallen Leaves II
PASSAGES DROPPED FROM
*LEAVES OF GRASS*

## from *Poets to Come*\*

Indeed, if it were not for you, what would I be?
What is the little I have done, except to arouse you?
I depend on being realized, long hence, where the broad
      fat prairies spread, and thence to Oregon and
      California inclusive,
I expect that the Texan and the Arizonian, ages hence,
      will understand me,
I expect that the future Carolinian and Georgian will
      understand me and love me,
I expect that Kanadians, a hundred, and perhaps many
      hundred years from now, in winter, in the splendor
      of the snow and woods, or on the icy lakes, will
      take me with them, and permanently enjoy
      themselves with me.

Of to-day I know I am momentary, untouched—I am
      the bard of the future....

---

\*Originally followed line 4 of "Poets to Come" as published in the 1860
edition. .

## from *By Blue Ontario's Shore**

An American literat fills his own place,
He justifies science—did you think the demonstrable
    less divine than the mythical?
He stands by liberty according to the compact of the
    first day of the first year of These States,
He concentrates in the real body and soul, and in the
    pleasure of things,
He possesses the superiority of genuineness over fiction
    and romance,
As he emits himself, facts are showered over with light,
The day-light is lit with more volatile light—the deep
    between the setting and rising sun goes deeper
    many fold,
Each precise object, condition, combination, process,
    exhibits a beauty—the multiplication-table its, old
    age its, the carpenter's trade its, the grand-opera its,
The huge-hulled clean-shaped Manhattan clipper at sea,
    under stream or full sail, gleams with unmatched
    beauty,
The national circles and large harmonies of government
    gleam with theirs,
The commonest definite intentions and actions with
    theirs.

---

*These lines come towards the end of Section 10 of "By Blue Ontario's
Shore," following the line: "He sees eternity in men and women, he does
not see men as dream or dots." They only appeared in the 1856 edition. In
1867, Whitman added the three line stanza beginning "For the great Idea,"
which took the place of this stanza.

# from *By Blue Ontario's Shore**

Language-using controls the rest;
Wonderful is language!
Wondrous the English language, language of live men,
Language of ensemble, powerful language of resistance,
Language of a proud and melancholy stock, and of all
    who aspire,
Language of growth, faith, self-esteem, rudeness,
    justice, friendliness, amplitude, prudence, decision,
    exactitude, courage,
Language to well-nigh express the inexpressible,
Language for the modern, language for America.


# from *Song of the Broad-Axe***

His shape arises,
Arrogant, masculine, näive, rowdyish,
Laugher, weeper, worker, idler, citizen, countryman,
Saunterer of woods, stander upon hills, summer
    swimmer in rivers or by the sea,
Of pure American breed, of reckless health, his body
    perfect, free from taint from top to toe, free forever
    from headache and dyspepsia, clean-breathed,

---

*In the 1856 edition, these lines concluded section 10 of "By Blue
Ontario's Shore."
**In the 1856 Leaves, this was the second stanza of Section 11 of "Song of
the Broad-Axe."

Ample-limbed, a good feeder, weight a hundred and
    eighty pounds, full-blooded, six feet high, forty
    inches around the breast and back,
Countenance sun-burnt, bearded, calm, unrefined,
Reminder of animals, meeter of savage and gentleman
    on equal terms,
Attitudes lithe and erect, costume free, neck gray and
    open, of slow movement on foot,
Passer of his right arm round the shoulders of his
    friends, companion of the street,
Persuader always of people to give him their sweetest
    touches, and never their meanest,
A Manhattanese bred, fond of Brooklyn, fond of
    Broadway, fond of the life of the wharves and the
    great ferries,
Enterer everywhere, welcomed everywhere, easily
    understood after all,
Never offering others, always offering himself,
    corroborating his phrenology,
Voluptuous, inhabitive, combative, conscientious,
    alimentive, intuitive, of copious friendship,
    sublimity, firmness, self-esteem, comparison,
    individuality, form, locality, eventuality,
Avowing by life, manners, works, to contribute
    illustrations of results of The States,
Teacher of the unquenchable creed, namely, egotism,
Inviter of others continually henceforth to try their
    strength against his.

## from *On the Beach at Night Alone**

What can the future bring me more than I have?
Do you suppose I wish to enjoy life in other spheres?

I say distinctly I comprehend no better sphere than this
    earth,
I comprehend no better life than the life of my body.

I do not know what follows the death of my body,
But I know well that whatever it is, it is best for me,
And I know well that whatever is really Me shall live just
    as much as before.

I am not uneasy but I shall have good housing to myself,
But this is my first—how can I like the rest any better?
Here I grew up—the studs and rafters are grown parts
    of me.

I am not uneasy but I am to be beloved by young and
    old men, and to love them the same,
I suppose the pink nipples of the breasts of women with
    whom I shall sleep will touch the side of my face
    the same,
But this is the nipple of a breast of my mother, always
    near and always divine to me, her true child and
    son, whatever comes.

---

*In the 1856 edition, these were the fourth through ninth stanzas of "On
the Beach at Night Alone."

I suppose I am to be eligible to visit the stars, in my
time,
I suppose I shall have myriads of new experiences—and
that the experience of this earth will prove only one
out of myriads;
But I believe my body and my Soul already indicate
those experiences,
And I believe I shall find nothing in the stars more
majestic and beautiful than I have already found on
the earth,
And I believe I have this night a clew through the
universes,
And I believe I have this night thought a thought of the
clef of eternity.

## from *To a Historian**

Advancing, to give the spirit and the traits of new
Democratic ages, myself, personally,
(Let the future behold them all in me—Me, so puzzling
and contradictory—Me, a Manhattanese, the most
loving and arrogant of men;)
I do not tell the usual facts, proved by records and
documents,
What I tell, (talking to every born American,) requires
no further proof than he or she who will hear me,
will furnish, by silently meditating alone;...

---

*These lines followed line 4 of "To a Historian" in the 1860 *Leaves*.

## from *Laws for Creations**

There they stand—I see them already, each poised and
	in its place,
Statements, models, censuses, poems, dictionaries,
	biographies, essays, theories—How complete! How
	relative and interfused! No one supersedes another;
They do not seem to me like the old specimens,
They seem to me like Nature at last, (America has given
	birth to them, and I have also;)
They seem to me at last as perfect as the animals, and as
	the rocks and weeds—fitted to them,
Fitted to the sky, to float with floating clouds—to rustle
	among the trees with rustling leaves,
To stretch with stretched and level waters, where ships
	silently sail in the distance.


## from *You Felons on Trial in Courts***

O bitter sprig! Confession sprig!
In the bouquet I give you place also—I bind you in,
Proceeding no further till, humbled publicly,
I give fair warning, once for all.

I own that I have been sly, thievish, mean, a
	prevaricator, greedy, derelict,

*These lines appeared after line 5 of "Laws for Creations" in 1860.
**In the first 1860 version, these were the first three stanzas of "You Felons
on Trial in Courts."

And I own that I remain so yet.

What foul thought but I think it—or have in me the
    stuff out of which it is thought?
What in darkness in bed at night, alone or with a
    companion?


## from *Out of the Cradle, Endlessly Rocking**

O a word! O what is my destination? (I fear it is
    henceforth chaos;)
O how joys, dreads, convolutions, human shapes, and all
    shapes, spring as from graves around me!
O phantoms, you cover all the land and all the sea!
O I cannot see in the dimness whether you smile or
    frown upon me;
O vapor, a look, a word! O well-beloved!
O you dear women's and men's phantoms!


## from *So Long!***

Yet not me, after all—let none be content with me,
I myself seek a man better than I am, or a woman better
    than I am,

---

*In 1860, these lines followed line 159 of "Out of the Cradle, Endlessly
Rocking": "O if I am to have so much let me have more."
**"So Long" was a very heavily revised poem. These 1860 stanzas origi-
nally followed line 8.

I invite defiance, and to make myself superseded,
All I have done, I would cheerfully give to be trod under
    foot, if it might only be the soil of superior poems.

I have established nothing for good,
I have but established those things, till things farther
    onward shall be prepared to be established,
And I am myself the preparer of things farther onward...

## from *So Long!**

Once more I enforce you to give play to yourself—and
    not to depend on me, or on any one but yourself,
Once more I proclaim the whole of America for each
    individual, without exception.

As I have announced the true theory of the youth,
    manhood, womanhood, of The States, I adhere to
    it;
As I have announced myself on immortality, the body,
    procreation, hauteur, prudence,
As I joined the stern crowd that still confronts the
    President with menacing weapons—I adhere to all,
As I have announced each age for itself, this moment I
    set the example.

I demand the choicest edifices to destroy them;

---

*These three stanzas followed line 14 of "So Long" in the 1860 edition.

Room! room! for new far-planning draughtsmen and
 engineers!
Clear that rubbish from the building-spots and the
 paths!

# Manuscript Poems

## Pictures

In a little house pictures I keep, many pictures hanging
    suspended—It is not a fixed house,
It is round—it is but a few inches from one side of it to
    the other side,
But behold! it has room enough—in it, hundreds and
    thousands,—all the varieties;
—Here! do you know this? This is cicerone himself;
And here, see you, my own States—and here the world
    itself,
       bowling
             through the air;
       rolling
And there, on the walls hanging, portraits of women
    and men, carefully kept,
This is the portrait of my dear mother—and this of my
    father—and these of my brothers and sisters;
This, (I name every thing as it comes,) This is a
    beautiful statue, long lost, dark buried, but never
    destroyed—now found by me, and restored to the
    light;
There five men, a group of sworn friends, stalwart,
    bearded, determined, work their way together
    through all the troubles and impediments of the
    world;

115

And that is a magical wondrous mirror—long it lay
    clouded, but the cloud has passed away,
It is now a clean and bright mirror—it will show you all
    you can conceive of, all you wish to behold;
And that is a picture intended for Death—it is very
    beautiful—(what else is so beautiful as Death?)
There is represented the Day, full of effulgence—full of
    seminal lust and love—full of action, life, strength,
    aspiration,
And there the Night, with mystic beauty, full of love
    also, and full of greater life—the Night, showing
    where the stars are;
There is a picture of Adam in Paradise—side by side
    with him Eve, (the Earth's bride and the Earth's
    bridegroom;)
There is an old Egyptian temple—and again, a Greek
    temple, of white marble;
There are Hebrew prophets chanting, rapt, extatic—and
    here is Homer;
Here is one singing canticles in an unknown tongue,
    before the Sanskrit was,
And here a Hindu sage, with his recitative in Sanskrit;
And here the divine Christ expounds eternal truth—
    expounds the Soul,
And here he appears en-route to Calvary, bearing the
    cross—See you, the blood and sweat streaming
    down his face, his neck;
And here, behold, a picture of once imperial Rome, full
    of palaces—full of masterful warriors;

And here, the questioner, the Athenian of the classical
    time—Socrates, in the market place,
(O divine tongue! I too grow silent under your
    elenchus,
(O you with bare feet, and bulging belly! I saunter
    along, following you, and obediently listen;)
And here Athens itself,—it is a clear forenoon,
Young men, pupils, collect in the gardens of a favorite
    master, waiting for him.
Some, crowded in groups, listen to the harangues or
    arguments of the elder ones,
Elsewhere, single figures, undisturbed by the buzz
    around them, lean against pillars, or within
    recesses, meditating, or studying from manuscripts,
Here and there, couples or trios, young and old, clear-
    faced, and of perfect physique, walk with twined
    arms, in divine friendship, happy,
Till, beyond, the master appears advancing—his form
    shows above the crowd, a head taller than they,
His gait is erect, calm and dignified—his features are
    colossal—he is old, yet his forehead has no
    wrinkles,
Wisdom undisturbed, self-respect, fortitude unshaken,
    are in his expression, his personality;
Wait till he speaks—what God's voice is that, sounding
    from his mouth?
He places virtue and self-denial above all the rest,
He shows to what a glorious height the man may
    ascend,

He shows how independent one may be of fortune—
    how triumphant over fate;
—And here again, this picture tells a story of the
    Olympic games,
See you, the chariot races? See you, the boxers boxing,
    and the runners running?
See you, the poets off there reciting their poems and
    tragedies, to crowds of listeners?
—And here, (for I have all kinds,) here is Columbus
    setting sail from Spain on his voyage of discovery;
This again is a series after the great French revolution,
This is the taking of the Bastile, the prison—this is the
    execution of the king.
This is the queen on her way to the scaffold—those are
    guillotines;
But this opposite, (abruptly changing,) is a picture from
    the prison-ships of my old city—Brooklyn city;
And now a merry recruiter passes, with fife and drum,
    seeking who will join his troop;
And there is an old European martyrdom—See you, the
    cracking fire—See the agonized contortions of the
    limbs, and the writhing of the lips! See the head
    thrown back;
And here is a picture of triumph—a General has
    returned, after a victory—the city turns out to meet
    him,
And here is a portrait of the English king, Charles the
    First, (are you a judge of physiognomy?)
And here is a funeral procession in the country,

A beloved daughter is carried in her coffin—there
    follow the parents and neighbors;
And here, see you—here walks the Boston truckman, by
    the side of his string-team—see the three horses,
    pacing stately, sagacious, one ahead of another;
—And this—whose picture is this?
Who is this, with rapid feet, curious, gay—going up and
    down Mannahatta, through the streets, along the
    shores, working his way through the crowds,
    observant and singing?
And this head of melancholy Dante, poet of penalties—
    poet of hell;
But this is a portrait of Shakespear, limner of feudal
    European lords (here are my hands, my brothers—
    one for each of you;)
—And there are wood-cutters, cutting down trees in my
    north east woods—see you, the axe uplifted;
And that is a picture of a fish-market—see there the
    shad, flat-fish, the large halibut,—there a pile of
    lobsters, and there another of oysters;
Opposite, a drudge in the kitchen, working, tired—and
    there again the laborer, in stained clothes, sour-
    smelling, sweaty—and again black persons and
    criminals;
And there the frivolous person—and there a crazy
    enthusiast—and there a young man lies sick of a
    fever, and is soon to die;
This, again, is a Spanish bull-fight—see, the animal with
    bent head, fiercely advancing;

And here, see you, a picture of a dream of despair, (—is
   it unsatisfied love?)
Phantoms, countless, men and women, after death,
   wandering;
And there are flowers and fruits—see the grapes, decked
   off with vine-leaves;
But see this!—see where graceful and stately the young
   queen-cow walks at the head of a large drove,
   leading the rest;
And there are building materials—brick, lime, timber,
   paint, glass, and iron, (so now you can build what
   you like;)
And this black portrait—this head, huge, frowning,
   sorrowful—is Lucifer's portrait—the denied God's
   portrait,
(But I do not deny him—though cast out and rebellious,
   he is my God as much as any;)
And again the heads of three other Gods—the God
   Beauty, the God Beneficence, and the God
   Universality, (they are mine, also;)
And there an Arab caravan, halting—See you, the palm
   trees, the camels, and the stretch of hot sand far
   away;
And there are my woods of Kanada, in winter, with ice
   and snow,
And here my Oregon hunting-hut, See me emerging
   from the door, bearing my rifle in my hand;
But there, see you, a reminiscence from over sea—a
   very old Druid, walking the woods of Albion;

And there, singular, on ocean waves, downward,
    buoyant, swift, over the waters, an occupied coffin
    floating;
And there, rude grave-mounds in California—and there
    a path worn in the grass,
And there hang painted scenes from my Kansas life—
    and there from what I saw in the Lake Superior
    region;
And here mechanics work in their shops, in towns—
    There the carpenter shoves his jack-plane—there
    the blacksmith stands by his anvil, leaning on his
    upright hammer;
This is Chicago with railroad depots, with trains
    arriving and departing—and, in their places,
    immense stores of grain, meat, and lumber;
And here are my slave-gangs, South, at work upon the
    roads, the women indifferently with the men—see,
    how clumsy, hideous, black, pouting, grinning, sly,
    besotted, sensual, shameless;
And this of a scene afar in the North, the arctic—those
    are the corpses of lost explorers, (no chaplets of
    roses will ever cap their icy graves—but I put a
    chaplet in this poem, for you, you sturdy English
    heros;)
But here, now copious—see you, here, the Wonders of
    eld, the famed Seven,
The Olympian statue this, and this the Artemesian
    tomb,
Pyramid this, Pharos this, and this the shrine of Diana,

These Babylon's gardens, and this Rhodes' high-lifted
　　marvel,
(But for all that, nigh at hand, see a wonder beyond any
　　of them,
Namely yourself—the form and thoughts of a man,
A man! because all the world, and all the inventions of
　　the world are but the food of the body and the soul
　　of one man;)
And here, while ages have grown upon ages,
Pictures of youths and greybeards, Pagan, and Jew, and
　　Christian,
Some retiring to caves—some in schools and piled
　　libraries,
To pore with ceaseless fervor over the myth of the
　　Infinite,
But ever recoiling, Pagan and Jew and Christian,
As from a haze, more dumb and thick than vapor above
　　the hot sea;
—And here now, (for all varieties, I say, hang in this
　　little house,)
A string of my Iroquois, aborigines—see you, where
　　they march in single file, without noise, very
　　cautious, through passages in the old woods;

　　Picture

O a husking-frolic in the West—see you, the large rude
　　barn—see you, young and old, laughing and joking,
　　as they husk the ears of corn;

And there in a city, a stormy political meeting—a torch-
light procession—candidates avowing themselves
to the people;
And here is the Lascar I noticed once in Asia—here he
remains still, pouring money into the sea, as an
offering to demons, for favor;
And there, in the midst of a group, a quell'd revolted
slave, cowering,
See you, the hand-cuffs, the hopple, and the blood-
stain'd cowhide;
And there hang, side by side, certain close comrades of
mine—a Broadway stage-driver, a lumberman of
Maine, and a deck-hand of a Mississippi steamboat;
And again the young man of Mannahatta, the celebrated
rough,
(The one I love well—let others sing whom they may—
him I sing for a thousand years!)
And there a historic piece—see you, where Thomas
Jefferson of Virginia sits reading Rousseau, the
Swiss, and compiling the Declaration of
Independence, the American compact;
And there, tall and slender, stands Ralph Waldo
Emerson, of New England, at the lecturer's desk
lecturing,
And there is my Congress in session in the Capitol—
there are my two Houses in session;
And here, behold two war-ships, saluting each other—
behold the smoke, bulging, spreading in round
clouds from the guns and sometimes hiding the
ships;

And there, on the level banks of the James river in
    Virginia stand the mansions of the planters;
And here an old black man, stone-blind, with a placard
    on his hat, sits low at the corner of a street,
    begging, humming hymn-tunes nasally all day to
    himself and receiving small gifts;
And this, out at sea, is a signal-bell—see you, where it is
    built on a reef, and ever dolefully keeps tolling, to
    warn mariners;
And this pictures shows what once happened in one of
    Napoleon's greatest battles,
(The tale was conveyed to me by an old French soldier,)
In the height of the roar and carnage of the battle, all of
    a sudden, from some unaccountable cause, the
    whole fury of the opposing armies subsided—there
    was a perfect calm,
It lasted almost a minute—not a gun was fired—all was
    petrified,
It was more solemn and awful than all the roar and
    slaughter;
—And here, (for still I name them as they come,) here
    are my timber-towers, guiding logs down a stream
    in the North;
And here a glimpse of my treeless llanos, where they
    skirt the Colorado, and sweep for a thousand miles
    on either side of the Rocky Mountains;

And there, on the whaling ground, in the Pacific, is a
    sailor, perched at the top-mast head, on the look
    out,
(You can almost hear him crying out, *There-e-'s white
    water, or The-e-re's black skin;*)
But here, (look you well,) see here the phallic choice of
    America, a full-sized man or woman—a natural,
    well-trained man or woman
(The phallic choice of America leaves the finesse of
    cities, and all the returns of commerce or
    agriculture, and the magnitude of geography, and
    achievements of literature and art, and all the
    shows of exterior victory, to enjoy the breeding of
    full-sized men, or one full-sized man or woman,
    unconquerable and simple;)
—For all those have I in a round house hanging—such
    pictures have I—and they are but little.
For whatever I have been, has afforded me superb
    pictures.
And whatever I have heard has given me perfect
    pictures,
And every hour of the day and night has given me
    copious pictures,
And every rod of land or sea affords me, as long as I live,
    inimitable pictures.

## Poem of Existence*

We call one the past, and we call another the future
But both are alike the present
It is not the past, though we call it so,—nor the future,
    though we call it so,
All the while it is the present only—both future and past
    are the present only.—

The curious realities now everywhere—on the surface
    of the earth,—in the interior of the earth
What is it? Is it liquid fire? Are there living creatures in
    that? Is it fire? solid? Is there not toward the core,
    some vast strange stifling vacuum?—Is there
    anything in that vacuum? any kind of curious flying
    or floating life with its nature fitted?

The existence on the innumerable stars, with their
    varied degrees of perfection, climate, swiftness
—Some probably are but forming, not so advanced as
    the earth—(Some are no doubt more advanced—

There is intercommunion
One sphere cannot know another sphere,
(Communion of life is with life only, and of what is after
    life

---

*"Poem of Existence" was probably written in the early 1850s.

(Each sphere knows itself only, and cannot commune
    beyond itself,
Life communes only with life,
Whatever it is that follows death.

*Uncollected Prose*

# Walt Whitman and his Poems

An American bard at last! One of the roughs, large, proud, affectionate, eating, drinking, and breeding, his costume manly and free, his face sunburnt and bearded, his postures strong and erect, his voice bringing hope and prophecy to the generous races of young and old. We shall cease shamming and be what we really are. We shall start an athletic and defiant literature. We realize now how it is, and what was most lacking. The interior American republic shall also be declared free and independent.

For all our intellectual people, followed by their books, poems, novels, essays, editorials, lectures, tuitions and criticisms, dress by London and Paris modes, receive what is received there, obey the authorities, settle disputes by the old tests, keep out of rain and sun, retreat to the shelter of houses and schools, trim their hair, shave, touch not the earth barefoot, and enter not the sea except in a complete bathing dress. One sees unmistakably genteel persons, travelled, college-learned, used to be served by servants, conversing without heat or vulgarity, supported on chairs, or walking through handsomely carpeted parlours, or along shelves bearing well-bound volumes, and walls adorned with curtained and collared portraits, and china things, and nick-nacks. But where in American literature is the first show of America? Where are the gristle and beards, and broad breasts, and space, and ruggedness, and nonchalance, that the souls of the people love? Where is the tremendous outdoors of these states? Where is the majesty of the federal mother, seated with more than antique grace, calm, just, indulgent to her brood of children, calling them around her, regarding the little and the large, and the younger and the older, with perfect impartiality? Where is the vehement growth of our cities? Where is the spirit of the strong rich life of the American mechanic, farmer, sailor, hunter, and miner? Where is the huge composite of all other nations, cast in a fresher and brawnier matrix, passing adolescence, and needed this day, live and arrogant, to lead the marches of the world?

Self-reliant, with haughty eyes, assuming to himself all the attributes of his country, steps Walt Whitman into literature, talking like a man unaware that there was ever hitherto such a production as a book, or such a being as a writer. Every move of him has the free play of the muscle of one who never knew what it was to feel that he stood in the presence of a superior. Every word that falls from his mouth shows silent disdain and defiance of the old theories and forms. Every phrase announces new laws; not once do his lips unclose except in conformity with them. With light and rapid touch he first indicates impatience of outside control—the sturdy defiance of '76, and the war and peace, and the leader-

ship of Washington, and the formation of the constitu-
tion—the union always surrounded by blatherers and
always calm and impregnable—the perpetual coming of
immigrants—the wharf-hemmed cities and superior
marine—the unsurveyed interior—the log-houses and
clearings, and wild animals and hunters and trappers—
the fisheries, and whaling, and gold-digging—the end-
less gestation of new States—the convening of Congress
every December, the members coming up from all cli-
mates, and from the uttermost parts—the noble char-
acter of the free American workman and
workwoman—the fierceness of the people when well
roused—the ardor of their friendships—the large ama-
tiveness—the equality of the female with the male—the
Yankee swap—the New York firemen and the target
excursion—the southern plantation life—the character
of the northeast and of the northwest and southwest—
and the character of America and the American people
everywhere. For these the old usages of poets afford
Walt Whitman no means sufficiently fit and free, and he
rejects the old usages. The style of the bard that is
waited for, is to be transcendent and new. It is to be
indirect, and not direct or descriptive or epic. Its quality
is to go through these to much more. Let the age and
wars (he says) of other nations be chanted, and their eras
and characters be illustrated, and that finish the verse.
Not so (he continues) the great psalm of the republic.
Here the theme is creative and has vista. Here comes
one among the well-beloved stone cutters, and
announces himself, and plans with decision and science,

and sees the solid and beautiful forms of the future where there are now no solid forms.

The style of these poems, therefore, is simply their own style, just born and red. Nature may have given the hint to the author of the *Leaves of Grass*, but there exists no book or fragment of a book which can have given the hint to them. All beauty, he says, comes from beautiful blood and a beautiful brain. His rhythm and uniformity he will conceal in the roots of his verses, not to be seen of themselves, but to break forth loosely as lilacs on a bush, and take shapes compact, as the shapes of melons, or chestnuts, or pears.

The poems of the *Leaves of Grass* are twelve in number. Walt Whitman at first proceeds to put his own body and soul into the new versification:

I celebrate myself,
And what I assume you shall assume,
For every atom belonging to me as good belongs to you.

He leaves houses and their shuttered rooms, for the open air. He drops disguise and ceremony, and walks forth with the confidence and gayety of a child. For the old decorums of writing he substitutes his own decorums. The first glance out of his eyes electrifies him with love and delight. He will have the earth receive and return his affection; he will stay with it as the bridegroom stays with the bride. The cool-breath'd ground, the slumbering and liquid trees, the just-gone sunset, the vitreous pour of the full moon, the tender and growing night, he salutes and touches, and they touch him. The sea supports him, and hurries him off with its powerful and crooked fingers. Dash me with amorous wet! then, he says; I can repay you.

The rules of polite circles are dismissed with scorn. Your stale modesties, he seems to say, are filthy to such a man as I.

I believe in the flesh and the appetites,
Seeing hearing and feeling are miracles, and each part
    and tag of me is a miracle.

I do not press my finger across my mouth,
I keep as delicate around the bowels as around the head
    and heart,
Copulation is no more rank to me than death is.

No skulker or tea-drinking poet is Walt Whitman. He will bring poems to fill the days and nights—fit for men and women with the attributes of throbbing blood and flesh. The body, he teaches, is beautiful. Sex is also beautiful. Are you to be put down, he seems to ask, to that shallow level of literature and conversation that stops a man's recognizing the delicious pleasure of his sex, or a woman hers? Nature he proclaims inherently clean. Sex will not be put aside; it is a great ordination of the universe. He works the muscle of the male and the teeming fibre of the female throughout his writings, as wholesome realities, impure only by deliberate intention and effort. To men and women he says, You can have healthy and powerful breeds of children on no less terms than these of mine. Follow me, and there shall be taller and richer crops of humanity on the earth.

Especially in the *Leaves of Grass* are the facts of eternity and immortality largely treated. Happiness is no dream, and perfection is no dream. Amelioration is my lesson, he says with calm voice, and progress is my lesson and the lesson of all things. Then his persuasion becomes a taunt, and his love bitter and compulsory. With strong and steady call he addresses men. Come, he seems to say, from the midst of all that you have been your whole life surrounding yourself with. Leave all the preaching and teaching of others, and mind only these words of mine.

Long enough have you dreamed contemptible dreams,
Now I wash the gum from your eyes,
You must habit yourself to the dazzle of the light and of
     every moment of your life.

Long have you timidly waded, holding a plank by the
     shore,
Now I will you to be a bold swimmer,
To jump off into the midst of the sea, and rise again and
     nod to me and shout, and laughingly dash with
     your hair.

I am the teacher of athletes,
He that by me spreads a wider breast than my own
     proves the width of my own,

He most honors my style who learns under it to destroy
    the teacher.

The boy I love, the same becomes a man not through
    derived power but in his own right,
Wicked, rather than virtuous out of conformity or fear,
Fond of his sweetheart, relishing well his steak,
Unrequited love or a slight cutting him worse than a
    wound cuts,
First rate to ride, to fight, to hit the bull's eye, to sail a
    skiff, to sing a song or play on the banjo,
Preferring scars and faces pitted with smallpox over all
    latherers and those that keep out of the sun.

I teach straying from me, yet who can stray from me?
I follow you whoever you are from the present hour;
My words itch at your ears till you understand them.

I do not say these things for a dollar, or to fill up the
    time while I wait for a boat;

It is you talking just as much as myself...I act as the
    tongue of you,
It was tied in your mouth...in mine it begins to be
    loosened.

I swear I will never mention love or death inside a
    house,
And I swear I never will translate myself at all, only to
    him or her who privately stays with me in the open
    air.

The eleven other poems have each distinct purposes, curiously veiled. Theirs is no writer to be gone through with in a day or a month. Rather it is his pleasure to elude you and provoke you for deliberate purposes of his own.

Doubtless in the scheme this man has built for himself, the writing of poems is but a proportionate part of the whole. It is plain that public and private performance, politics, love, friendship, behavior, the art of conversation, science, society, the American people, the reception of the great novelties of city and country, all have their equal call upon him, and receive equal attention. In politics he could enter with the freedom and reality he shows in poetry. His scope of life is the amplest of any yet in philosophy. He is the true spiritualist. He recognizes no annihilation, or death, or loss of identity. He is the largest lover and sympathizer that has appeared in literature. He loves the earth and sun and the animals. He does not separate the learned from the unlearned, the northerner from the southerner, the white from the black, or the native from the immigrant just landed at the wharf. Every one, he seems to say, appears excellent to me; every employment is adorned, and every male and female glorious.

The press of my foot to the earth springs a hundred
    affections,
They scorn the best I can do to relate them.

I am enamored of growing outdoors,
Of men that live among cattle or taste of the ocean or
    woods,
Of the builders and steerers of ships, of the wielders of
    axes and mauls, of the drivers of horses,
I can eat and sleep with them week in and week out.

What is commonest and cheapest and nearest and
    easiest is Me,
Me going in for my chances, spending for vast returns,
Adorning myself to bestow myself on the first that will
    take me,
Not asking the sky to come down to my goodwill,
Scattering it freely forever.

If health were not his distinguishing attribute, this poet
would be the very harlot of persons. Right and left he
flings his arms, drawing men and women with undeni-
able love to his close embrace, loving the clasp of their
hands, the touch of their necks and breasts, and the
sound of their voices. All else seems to burn up under
his fierce affection for persons. Politics, religions, insti-
tutions, art, quickly fall aside before them. In the whole
universe, he says, I see nothing more divine than human
souls.

When the psalm sings instead of the singer,
When the script preaches instead of the preacher,
When the pulpit descends and goes instead of the carver
    that carved the supporting desk,

When the sacred vessels or the bits of the eucharist, or
    the lath and plast, procreate as effectually as the
    young silversmiths or bakers, or the masons in their
    overalls,
When a university course convinces like a slumbering
    woman and child convince,
When the minted gold in the vault smiles like the night-
    watchman's daughter,
When warrantee deeds loafe in chairs opposite and are
    my friendly companions,
I intend to reach them my hand and make as much of
    them as I make of men and women.

Who then is that insolent unknown? Who is it, praising
himself as if others were not fit to do it, and coming
rough and unbidden among writers, to unsettle what
was settled, and to revolutionize in fact our modern civ-
ilization? Walt Whitman was born on Long Island, on
the hills about thirty miles from the greatest American
city, on the last day of May 1819, and has grown up in
Brooklyn and New York to be thirty-six years old, to
enjoy perfect health, and to understand his country and
its spirit.

Interrogations more than this, and that will not be put
off unanswered, spring continually through the perusal
of *Leaves of Grass:*

    Must not the true American poet indeed absorb all
others, and present a new and far more ample and vig-
orous type?

Has not the time arrived for a school of life writing and tuition consistent with the principles of these poems? consistent with the free spirit of this age, and with the American truths of politics? consistent with geology, and astronomy, and phrenology, and human physiology? consistent with the sublimity of immortality and the directness of common sense?

If in this poem the United States have found their poetic voice and taken measure and form, is it any more than a beginning? Walt Whitman himself disclaims singularity in his work, and announces the coming after him of great successions of poets, and that he but lifts his finger to give the signal.

Was he not needed? Has not literature been bred in-and-in long enough? Has it not become unbearably artificial?

Shall a man of faith and practice in the simplicity of real things be called eccentric, while every disciple of the fictitious school writes without question?

Shall it still be the amazement of the light and dark that freshness of expression is the rarest quality of all?

You have come in good time, Walt Whitman! In opinions, in manners, in costumes, in books, in the aims and occupancy of life, in associates, in poems, conformity to all unnatural and tainted customs passes without remark, while perfect naturalness, health, faith, self-reliance, and all primal expressions of the manliest love and friendship, subject one to the stare and controversy of the world.

*United States Review*, September 1855

# An English and an American Poet

It is always reserved for second-rate poems immediately to gratify. As first-rate or natural objects, in their perfect simplicity and proportion, do not startle or strike, but appear no more than matters of course, so probably natural poetry does not, for all its being the rarest, and telling of the longest and largest work. The artist or writer whose talent is to please the connoisseurs of his time, may obey the laws of his time, and achieve the intense and elaborated beauty of parts, or to limit himself by any laws less than those universal ones of the great masters, which include all times, and all men and women, and the living and the dead. For from the study of the universe is drawn this irrefragable truth, that the law of the requisites of a grand poem, or any other complete workmanship, is originality, and the average and superb beauty of the ensemble. Possessed with this law, the fitness of aim, time, persons, places, surely follows. Possessed with this law, and doing justice to it, no poet or any one else will make anything ungraceful or mean, any more than any emanation of nature is.

The poetry of England, by the many rich geniuses of that wonderful little island, has grown out of the facts of the English race, the monarchy and aristocracy prominent over the rest, and conforms to the spirit of them. No nation ever did or ever will receive with national affection any poets except those born of its national blood. Of these, the writings express the finest infusions of government, traditions, faith, and the dependence or independence of a people, and even the good or bad physiognomy, and the ample or small geography. Thus what very properly fits a subject of the British crown may fit very ill an American freeman. No fine romance, no inimitable delineation of character, no grace of delicate illustrations, no rare picture of shore or mountain or sky, no deep thought of the intellect, is so important to a man as his opinion of himself is; everything receives its tinge from that. In the verse of all those undoubtedly great writers, Shakespeare just as much as the rest, there is the air which to America is the air of death. The mass of the people, the laborers and all who serve, are slag, refuse. The countenances of kings and great lords are beautiful; the countenances of mechanics are ridiculous and deformed. What play of Shakespeare, represented in America, is not an insult to America, to the marrow in its bones? How can the tone never silent in their plots and characters be applauded, unless Washington should have been caught and hung, and Jefferson was the most enormous of liars, and common persons, north and south, should bow low to their betters, and to organic superiority of blood? Sure as the heavens envelop the earth, if the Americans want a race of bards worthy of 1855, and of the stern reality of this republic, they must cast around for men essentially different from the old poets, and from the modern successions of jinglers and snivellers and fops.

English versification is full of these danglers, and America follows after them. Everybody writes poetry, and yet there is not a single poet. An age greater than the proudest of the past is swiftly slipping away, without one lyric voice to seize its greatness, and speak it as an encouragement and onward lesson. We have heard, by many grand announcements, that he was to come, but will he come?

A mighty Poet whom this age shall choose
To be its spokesman to all coming times.
In the ripe full-blown season of his soul,
He shall go forward in his spirit's strength,
And grapple with the questions of all time,
And wring from them their meanings. As King Saul
Called up the buried prophet from his grave
To speak his doom, so shall this Poet-king
Call up the dread past from its awful grave
To tell him of our future. As the air
Doth sphere the world, so shall his heart of love—
Loving mankind, not peoples. As the lake
Reflects the flower, tree, rock, and bending heaven,
Shall he reflect our great humanity;
And as the young Spring breathes with living breath
On a dead branch, till it sprouts fragrantly
Green leaves and sunny flowers, shall he breathe life
Through every theme he touch, making all Beauty
And Poetry forever like the stars.

                                        (Alexander Smith)

The best of the school of poets at present received in great Britain and America is Alfred Tennyson. He is the bard of ennui and of the aristocracy, and their combination into love. This love is the old stock love of playwrights and romancers, Shakespeare the same as the rest. It is possessed of the same unnatural and shocking passion for some girl or woman, that wrenches it from its manhood, emasculated and impotent, without strength to hold the rest of the objects and goods of life in their proper positions. It seeks nature for sickly uses. It goes screaming and weeping after the facts of the universe, in their calm beauty and equanimity, to note the occurrence of itself, and to sound the news, in connexion with the charms of the neck, hair, or complexion of a particular female.

Poetry, to Tennyson and his British and American eleves, is a gentleman of the first degree, boating, fishing, and shooting genteelly through nature, admiring the ladies, and talking to them, in company, with that elaborate half-choked deference that is to be made up by the terrible license of men among themselves. The spirit of the burnished society of upper-class England fills this writer and his effusions from top to toe. Like that, he does not ignore courage and the superior qualities of men, but all is to show forth through dandified forms. He meets the nobility and gentry halfway. The models are the same both to the poet and the parlors. Both have the same supercilious elegance, both love the reminiscences which extol caste, both agree on the topics proper for mention and discussion, both hold the same undertone of church and state, both have the same languishing melancholy and irony, both indulge largely in persiflage, both are marked by the contour of high blood and a constitutional aversion to anything cowardly and mean, both accept the love depicted in romances as the great business of a life or a poem, both seem unconscious of the mighty truths of eternity and immortality, both are silent on the presumptions of liberty and equality, and both devour themselves in solitary lassitude. Whatever may be said of all this, it harmonizes and represents facts. The present phases of high-life in Great Britain are as natural a growth there, as Tennyson and his poems are a natural growth of those phases. It remains to be distinctly admitted that this man is a real first-class poet, infused amid all that ennui and aristocracy.

Meanwhile a strange voice parts others aside and demands for its owner that position that is only allowed after the seal of many returning years has stamped with approving stamp the claims of the loftiest leading genius. Do you think the best honors of the earth are won so easily, Walt Whitman? Do you think city and country are to fall before the vehement egotism of your recitative of yourself?

I am the poet of the body,
And I am the poet of the soul.

The pleasures of heaven are with me, and the pains of
    hell are with me,
The first I graft and increase upon myself...the latter I
    translate into a new tongue.

I am the poet of the woman the same as the man,
And I say it is as great to be a woman as to be a man,
And I say there is nothing greater than the mother of
    men.

I chant a new chant of dilation or pride,
We have had ducking and deprecating about enough,
I show that size is only development.

It is indeed a strange voice! Critics and lovers and
readers of poetry as hitherto written, may well be
excused the chilly and unpleasant shudders which will
assuredly run through them, to their very blood and
bones, when they first read Walt Whitman's poems. If
this is poetry, where must its foregoers stand? And what
is at once to become of the ranks of rhymesters, melan-
choly and swallow-tailed, and of all the confectioners
and upholsters of verse, if the tan-faced man here
advancing and claiming to speak for America and the
nineteenth hundred of the Christian list of years, typi-
fies indeed the natural and proper bard?

    The theory and practice of poets have hitherto
been to select certain ideas or events or personages, and
then describe them in the best manner they could,
always with as much ornament as the case allowed. Such

are not the theory and practice of the new poet. He never presents for perusal a poem ready-made on the old models, and ending when you come to the end of it; but every sentence and every passage tells of an interior not always seen, and exudes an impalpable something which sticks to him that reads, and pervades and provokes him to tread the half-invisible road where the poet, like an apparition, is striding fearlessly before. If Walt Whitman's premises are true, then there is a subtler range of poetry than that of the grandeur of acts and events, as in Homer, or of characters, as in Shakespeare—poetry to which all other writing is subservient, and which confronts the very meanings of the works of nature and competes with them. It is the direct bringing of occurrences and persons and things to bear on the listener or beholder, to reappear through him or her; and it offers the best way of making them a part of him and her as the right aim of the greatest poet.

Of the spirit of life in visible forms—of the spirit of the seed growing out of the ground—of the spirit of the resistless motion of the globe passing unsuspected but quick as lightning along its orbit—of them is the spirit of this man's poetry. Like them it eludes and mocks criticism, and appears unerringly in results. Things, facts, events, persons, days, ages, qualities, tumble pellmell, exhaustless and copious, with what appear to be the same disregard of parts, and the same absence of special purpose, as in nature. But the voice of the few rare and controlling critics, and the voice of more than one generation of men, or two generations of men, must speak for the inexpressible purposes of nature, and for this haughtiest of writers that has ever yet written and printed a book. He is to prove either the most lamentable of failures or the most glorious of triumphs, in the known history of literature. And after all we have written we confess our brain-felt and heart-felt inability to decide which we think it is likely to be.

*American Phrenological Review*, October 1955

# An American Primer

## F O R E W O R D

"An American Primer" is a challenge rather than a fin-
ished fight. We find Whitman on this occasion rather
laying his plans than undertaking to perfect them. It
would be unfair to take such a mass of more or less dis-
jointed notes and pass them under severe review.
Whitman never intended them for publication. He
should not be criticized, as he has been by certain
American editors, for an act for which he is in no way
responsible. The "Primer" is not a dogma. It is an inter-
rogation. Even as a dogma something might be said for
it. As a question it intimates its own answer. One of
Whitman's remarks about it was this: "It does not sug-
gest the invention but describes the growth of an
American English enjoying a distinct identity."
Whitman would every now and then get on his financial
uppers. Then he would say: "I guess I will be driven to
the lecture field in spite of myself." The "Primer" was
one of his projected lecture themes. The lecture idea
had possessed him most convincingly in the period that
antedated our personal acquaintance. *Leaves of Grass*
appeared before I was born. When I got really into con-

tact with Whitman the fight was on in full fury. "The *Leaves* has always meant fight to the world. It never meant fight to me." That was what Whitman said of it. He would make a point of my youth. "You bring young blood to the field. We are veterans—we welcome you."

Whitman at different times, especially in the beginning, when he struck up his rebel note, planned for all sorts of literary ventures which were not consummated. Whitman was undoubtedly convinced that he had a mission. This conviction never assumed fanatic forms. Whitman was the most catholic man who ever thought he had a mission. But he did regard himself as such a depository. Yet he never believed or contended that he possessed exclusive powers or an extraordinary divination. He felt that if the message with which he was entrusted did not get out through him it would get out through some other. But in his earlier career, after he tired of writing in the formal way and to the formal effect—for he played the usual juvenile part in literary mimicry—he felt that it would be difficult, if not impossible, to secure publishers either for his detail work or for his books. He often asked himself: How am I to deliver my goods? And he told me that when the idea of "An American Primer" originally came to him it was for a lecture. Yet these notes in themselves were only fragments. He never looked upon them as furnishing more than a start. "They might make the material for a good talk," he said. "It's only a sketch-piece anyway," he said again: "a few rough touches here and there, not rounding up the theme—rather showing what may be made of it. I often think the *Leaves* themselves are much the same sort of thing: a passageway to something rather than a thing in itself concluded: not the best that might be done but the best it is necessary to do for the present, to break the ground."

Whitman wrote at this "Primer" in the early fifties. And there is evidence that he made brief additions to it from time to time in the ten years that followed. The most of the manuscript notes are scribbled on sheets of various tints improvised from the paper covers used on the unbound copies of the 1855 edition. There is later paper and later handwriting. But the notes were largely written in the rather exciting five years before the war. "That stretch of time after 1855 until 1861 was crowded with personal as well as political preparations for war." But after he had issued the first edition of *Leaves of Grass*, and after he found the book surviving into the 1856 and 1860 editions, some of his old plans, this lecture scheme among them, were abandoned. The "Primer" was thenceforth, as a distinct project, held in abeyance. I remember that in the late eighties he said to me: "I may yet bring the 'Primer' out." And when I laughed incredulously he added: "Well, I guess you are right to laugh: I suppose I never shall. And the best of the 'Primer' stuff has no doubt leaked into my other work." It is indeed true that Whitman gave expression to the substance of the 'Primer' in one way or another. Even some of its sentences are utilized here and there in his prose and verse volumes.

In referring to the "Primer" upon another occasion, Whitman said: "This subject of language interests me—interests me: I never quite get it out of my mind. I sometimes think the *Leaves* is only a language experiment—that it is an attempt to give the spirit, the body, the man, new words, new potentialities of speech—an American, a cosmopolitan (the best of America is the best cosmopolitanism) range of self-expression. The new world, the new times, the new peoples, the new vista, need a tongue according—yes, what is more, will have such a tongue—will not be satisfied until it is evolved." But the study brought to bear upon the subject in the manuscript now under view was never resumed. The "Primer," therefore, is, as a part of Whitman's serious literary product, of marked significance. Whitman said of it: "It was first intended for a lecture: then when I gave up the idea of lecturing it was intended for a book: now, as it stands, it is neither a lecture nor a book."

As an alternate to his adopted headline I find this among Whitman's memoranda: "The Primer of Words: For American Young Men and Women, For Literati, Orators, Teachers, Musicians, Judges, Presidents, &c."

I have followed the original manuscript without any departures whatever. All its peculiarities of capitalization and punctuation are allowed to remain untouched.

Horace Traubel

# An American Primer

Much is said of what is spiritual, and of spirituality, in this, that, or the other—in objects, expressions.—For me, I see no object, no expression, no animal, no tree, no art, no book, but I see, from morning to night, and from night to morning, the spiritual.—Bodies are all spiritual.—All words are spiritual—nothing is more spiritual than words.—Whence are they? along how many thousands and tens of thousands of years have they come? those eluding, fluid, beautiful, fleshless, realities, Mother, Father, Water, Earth, Me, This, Soul, Tongue, House, Fire.

A great observation will detect sameness through all languages, however old, however new, however polished, however rude.—As humanity is one under its amazing diversities, language is one under its.—The flippant read on some long past age, wonder at its dead costumes [customs?], its amusements, &c.; but the master understands well the old, ever-new, ever-common grounds, below those annual growths.—The master, I say, between any two ages, any two languages and two humanities, however wide apart in time and space, marks well not the superficial shades of difference, but the mass-shades of a joint nature.

In a little while, in the United States, the English language, enriched with contributions from all languages, old and new, will be spoken by a hundred millions of people:—perhaps a hundred thousand words ("seventy or eighty thousand words"—Noah Webster, of the English language).

The Americans are going to be the most fluent and melodious voiced people in the world—and the most perfect users of words.—Words follow character—nativity, independence, individuality.

I see that the time is nigh when the etiquette of saloons is to be discharged from that great thing, the renovated English speech in America.—The occasions of the English speech in America are immense, profound—stretch over ten thousand vast cities, over millions of miles of meadows, farms, mountains, men, through thousands of years—the occasions of saloons are for a coterie, a bon soir or two,—involve waiters standing behind chairs, silent, obedient, with backs that can bend and must often bend.

What beauty there is in words! What a lurking curious charm in the sound of some words! Then voices! Five or six times in a lifetime, (perhaps not so often,) you have heard from men and women such voices, as they spoke the most common word!—What can it be that from those few men and women made so much out of the most common word! Geography, shipping, steam, the mint, the electric telegraph, railroads, and so forth, have many strong and beautiful words. Mines—iron works—the sugar plantations of

Louisiana—the cotton crop and the rice crop—Illinois wheat—Ohio corn and pork—Maine lumber—all these sprout in hundreds and hundreds of words, all tangible and clean-lived, all having texture and beauty.

To all thoughts of your or any one's mind—to all yearnings, passions, love, hate, ennui, madness, desperation of men for women, and of women for men,—to all charging and surcharging—that head which poises itself on your neck and is electric in the body beneath your head, or runs with the blood through your veins—or in those curious incredible miracles you call eyesight and hearing—to all these, and the like of these, have been made words.—Such are the words that are never new and never old.

What a history is folded, folded inward and inward again, in the single word I.

The *words of the Body!* The words of Parentage! The words of Husband and Wife. The words of Offspring! The word Mother! The word Father!

The words of *Behaviour* are quite numerous.— They follow the law; they are courteous, grave, have polish, have a sound of presence, and abash all furniture and shallowness out of their sight.

*The words* of maternity are all the words that were ever spoken by the mouth of man, the child of woman— but they are reborn words, and the mouth of the full-sized mother, daughter, wife, amie, does not offend by using any one of them.

*Medicine* has hundreds of useful and characteristic words—new means of cure—new schools of doctors—

the wonderful anatomy of the body—the names of a thousand diseases—surgeon's terms—hydropathy—all that relates to the great organs of the body.—The medical art is always grand—nothing affords a nobler scope for superior men and women.—It, of course, will never cease to be near to man, and add new terms.

Law, (Medicine) Religion, the Army, the personnel of the Army and Navy, the Arts, stand on their old stock of words, without increase.—In the law, is to be noticed a growing impatience with formulas, and with diffuseness, and, venerable slang. The personnel of the Army and the Navy exists in America, apart from the throbbing life of America—an exile in the land, foreign to the instincts and tastes of the people, and, of course, soon in due time to give place to something native, something warmed with throbs of our own life.

These States are rapidly supplying themselves with new words, called for by new occasions, new facts, new politics, new combinations.—Far plentier additions will be needed, and, of course, will be supplied.

(Because it is a truth that) the words continually used among the people are, in numberless cases, not the words used in writing, or recorded in the dictionaries by authority.—There are just as many words in daily use, not inscribed in the dictionary, and seldom or never in any print.—Also, the forms of grammar are never persistently obeyed, and cannot be.

The Real Dictionary will give all words that exist in use, the bad words as well as any.—The Real Grammar will be that which declares itself a nucleus of the spirit of the laws, with liberty to all to carry out the spirit of the laws, even by violating them, if necessary.—The English Language is grandly lawless like the race who use it—or, rather, breaks out of the little laws to enter truly the higher ones. It is so instinct with that which underlies laws, and the purports of laws, it refuses all petty interruptions in its way.

*Books* themselves have their peculiar words— namely, those that are never used in living speech in the real world, but only used in the world of books.— Nobody ever actually talks as books and plays talk.

The Morning has its words, and the Evening has its words.—How much there is in the word Light!—How vast, surrounding, falling, sleepy, noiseless, is the word Night!—It hugs with unfelt yet living arms.

Character makes words.—The English stock, full enough of faults, but averse to all folderol, equable, instinctively just, latent with pride and melancholy, ready with brawned arms, with free speech, with the knife-blade for tyrants and the reached hand for slaves,—have put all these in words.—We have them in America,—they are the body of the whole of the past.— We are to justify our inheritance—we are to pass it on to those who are to come after us, a thousand years hence, as we have grown out of the English of a thousand years ago: American geography,—the plenteousness and variety of the great nations of the Union—the thousands of settlements—the seacoast—the Canadian north—the Mexican south—California and Oregon— the inland seas—the mountains—Arizona—the prairies—the immense rivers.

Many of the slang words among fighting men, gamblers, thieves, prostitutes, are powerful words. These words ought to be collected—the bad words as well as the good.—Many of these bad words are fine.

Music has many good words, now technical, but of such rich and juicy character that they ought to be taken for common use in writing and speaking.

New forms of science, newer freer characters, may have something in them to need new words.—One beauty of words is exactitude.—To me each word out of the——that now compose the English language, has its own meaning, and does not stand for anything but itself—and there are no two words the same any more than there are two persons the same.

Much of America is shown in its newspaper names, and in the names of its steamboats, ships—names of characteristic amusements and games.

What do you think words are? Do you think words are positive and original things in themselves?—No: Words are not original and arbitrary in themselves.— Words are a result—they are the progeny of what has been or is in vogue.—If iron architecture comes in vogue, as it seems to be coming, words are wanted to stand for all about iron architecture, for the work it causes, for the different branches of work and of the workman—those blocks of buildings, seven stories high, with light strong façades, and girders that will not crumble a mite in a thousand years.

Also words to describe all American peculiarities,— the splendid and rugged characters that are forming among these states, or are already formed—in the cities, the firemen of Mannahatta and the target excursionist and Bowery boy—the Boston truckman—the Philadelphian.—

In America an immense number of new words are needed, to embody the new political facts, the compact of the Declaration of Independence, and of the Constitution—the union of the States—the new States—the Congress—the modes of election—the stump speech—the ways of electioneering—addressing the people—stating all that is to be said in modes that fit the life and experience of the Indianian, the Michiganian, the Vermonter, the men of Maine—also words to answer the modern, rapidly spreading, faith, of the vital equality of women with men, and that they are to be placed on an exact plane, politically, socially, and in business, with men. Words are wanted to supply the copious trains of facts, and flanges of facts, feelings, arguments, and adjectival facts, growing out of all new knowledges. Phrenology.

Drinking brandy, gin, beer, is generally fatal to the perfection of the voice;—meanness of mind the same;—gluttony in eating, of course the same; a thinned habit of body, or a rank habit of body—masturbation, inordinate going with women, rot the voice. Yet no man can have a great vocation who has no experience with women and no woman who has no experience with men. The final fiber and charm of the voice follows the chaste drench of love.

The great Italian singers are above all others in the world from causes quite the same as those that make the voices of the native healthy substrata of Mannahatta young men, especially the drivers of horses and all whose work leads to free loud calling and commanding, have such a ring and freshness.

Pronunciation of Yankees is nasal and offensive—it has the flat tones.—It could probably be changed by placing only those teachers in schools who have rich ripe voices—and by the children practicing to speak from the chest and in the guttural and baritone (methods) voice. All sorts of physical, moral, and mental deformities are inevitably returned in the voice.

The races that in their realities are supple, obedient, cringing, have hundreds of words to express hundreds of forms of acts, thoughts, flanges, of those realities, which the English tongue knows nothing of.

The English tongue is full of strong words native or adopted to express the blood-born passion of the race for rudeness and resistance, as against polish and all acts to give in: robust, brawny, athletic, muscular, acrid, harsh, rugged, severe, pluck, grit, effrontery, stern, resistance, bracing, rude, rugged, rough, shaggy, bearded, arrogant, haughty. These words are alive and sinewy—they walk, look, step with an air of command.—They will often lead the rest—they will not follow.—How can they follow?—They will appear strange in company unlike themselves.

English words.—Even people's names were spelt by themselves, sometimes one way sometimes another.—

Public necessity remedies all troubles.—Now, in the 80th year of These States, there is a little diversity in the ways of spelling words, and much diversity in the ways of pronouncing them;—steamships, railroads, newspapers, submarine telegraphs, will probably bring them in.—If not, it is not important.

So in the accents and inflections of words.— Language must cohere—it cannot be left loosely to float or to fly away.—Yet all the rules of the accents and inflections of words, drop before a perfect voice—that may follow the rules or be ignorant of them—it is indifferent which.—Pronunciation is the stamina of language,—it is language.—The noblest pronunciation, in a city or race, marks the noblest city or race, or descendants thereof.

Why are names (words) so mighty?—Because facts, ancestry, maternity, faiths, are.—Slowly, sternly, inevitably, move the souls of the earth, and names (words) are its (their) signs.

Kosmos words, Words of the *Free Expansion of Thought, History, Chronology, Literature*, are showing themselves, with foreheads, muscular necks and breasts.—These gladden me.—I put my arms around them—touch my lips to theirs. The past hundred centuries have confided much to me, yet they mock me, frowning.—I think I am done with many of the words of the past hundred centuries.—I am mad that their poems, bibles, words, still rule and represent the earth, and are not yet superseded.—But why do I say so?—I must not, will not, be impatient.

In American city excursions, for military practice, for firing at the target, for all the exercises of health and manhood—why should not women accompany them?— I expect to see the time in Politics, Business, Public Gatherings, Processions, Excitements, when women shall not be divided from men, but shall take their part on the same terms as men. What sort of women have Massachusetts, Ohio, Virginia, Pennsylvania, and the rest, correspondent with what they continually want? Sometimes I have fancied that only from superior, hardy women can rise the future superiorities of These States.

*Man's words*, for the young men of these states, are all words that have arisen out of the qualities of mastership, going first, brunting danger first,—words to identify a hardy boyhood—knowledge—an erect, sweet, lusty, body, without taint—choice and chary of its love-power.

The spelling of words is subordinate.—Morbidness for nice spelling, and tenacity for or against some one letter or so, means dandyism and impotence in literature.—Of course the great writers must have digested all these things,—passed lexicons, etymologies, orthographies, through them and extracted the nutriment.—Modern taste is for brevity and for ranging words in spelling classes;—probably, the words of the English tongue can never be ranged in spelling classes. The Phonetic (?) Spelling is on natural principles—it has arbitrary forms of letters and combinations of letters, for all sounds.—It may in time prevail—it surely will prevail if it is best it should.—For many hundred years there was nothing like settled spelling.

A perfect user of words uses things—they exude in power and beauty from him—miracles from his hands— miracles from his mouth—lilies, clouds, sunshine, woman, poured copiously—things, whirled like chain- shot rocks, defiance, compulsion, houses, iron, locomo- tives, the oak, the pine, the keen eye, the hairy breast, the Texan ranger, the Boston truckman, the woman that arouses a man, the man that arouses a woman.

Tavern words, such as have reference to drinking, or the compliments of those who drink—the names of some three hundred different American tavern-drinks in one part or another of These States.

Words of all degrees of dislike, from just a tinge, onward or deepward.

Words of approval, admiration, friendship. This is to be said among the young men of 'These States, that with a wonderful tenacity of friendship, and passionate fondness for their friends, and always a manly readiness to make friends, they yet have remarkably few words of names for the friendly sentiments.—They seem to be words that do not thrive here among the muscular classes, where the real quality of friendship is always freely to be found.—Also, they are words which the muscular classes, the young men of these states, rarely use, and have an aversion for;—they never give words to their most ardent friendships.

*Words of politics* are numerous in these states, and many of them peculiar.—The western states have terms of their own: the President's message—the political meeting—the committees—the resolutions: new vegeta- bles—new trees—new animals.

If success and breed follow the camels and drome-
daries, that are now just introduced into Texas, to be
used for travel and traffic over the vast wilds between
the lower Mississippi and the Pacific, a number of new
words will also have to be tried after them.

The appetite of the people of These States, in pop-
ular speeches and writings, is for unhemmed latitude,
coarseness, directness, live epithets, expletives, words of
opprobrium, resistance.—This I understand because I
have the taste myself as large as largely as any one.—I
have pleasure in the use, on fit occasions, of traitor,
coward, liar, shyster, skulk, doughface, trickster, mean
curse, backslider, thief, impotent, lickspittle.

The great writers are often select of their audi-
ences.—The greatest writers only are well-pleased and
at their ease among the unlearned—are received by
common men and women familiarly, do not hold out
obscure, but come welcome to table, bed, leisure, by day
and night.

A perfect writer would make words sing, dance,
kiss, do the male and female act, bear children, weep,
bleed, rage, stab, steal, fire cannon, steer ships, sack
cities, charge with cavalry or infantry, or do any thing,
that man or woman or the natural powers can do.

Latent, in a great user of words, must actually be all
passions, crimes, trades, animals, stars, God, sex, the
past, might, space, metals, and the like—because these
are the words, and he who is not these, plays with a for-
eign tongue, turning helplessly to dictionaries and
authorities.—How can I tell you?—I put many things

on record that you will not understand at first—perhaps not in a year—but they must be (are to be) understood.—The earth, I see, writes with prodigal clear hands all summer, forever, and all winter also, content, and certain to be understood in time—as, doubtless, only the greatest user of words himself fully enjoys and understands himself.

Words of Names of Places are strong, copious, unruly, in the repertoire for American pens and tongues. The Names of These States—the names of Countries, Cities, Rivers, Mountains, Villages, Neighborhoods— poured plentifully from each of the languages that graft the English language—or named from some natural peculiarity of water or earth, or some event that happened there—often named, from death, from some animal, from some of those subtle analogies that the common people are so quick to perceive.—The names in the list of the Post Offices of These States are studies. What name a city has—What name a State, river, sea, mountain, wood, prairie, has—is no indifferent matter.—All aboriginal names sound good. I was asking for something savage and luxuriant, and behold here are the aboriginal names. I see how they are being preserved. They are honest words—they give the true length, breadth, depth. They all fit. Mississippi!—the word winds with chutes—it rolls a stream three thousand miles long. Ohio, Connecticut, Ottawa, Monongahela, all fit.

*Names* are magic.—One word can pour such a flood through the soul.—To-day I will mention Christ's before all other names.—Grand words of names are still left.—What is it that flows through me at the sight of the word Socrates, or Cincinnatus, or Alfred of the olden time—or at the sight of the word Columbus, or Shakespeare, or Rousseau, or Mirabeau—or at the sight of the word Washington, or Jefferson, or Emerson?

Out of Christ are divine words—out of this savior. Some words are fresh-smelling, like lilies, roses, to the soul, blooming without failure.—The name of Christ—all words that have arisen from the life and death of Christ, the divine son, who went about speaking perfect words, no patois—whose life was perfect,—the touch of whose hands and feet was miracles—who was cruci-fied—his flesh laid in a shroud, in the grave.*

Words of Names of Persons, thus far, still return the old continents and races—return the past three thousand years—perhaps twenty thousand—return the Hebrew Bible, Greece, Rome, France, the Goths, the Celts, Scandinavia, Germany, England. Still questions come: What flanges are practicable for names of persons that mean These States?—What is there in the best aboriginal names? What is there in strong words of qualities, bodily, mental,—a name given to the cleanest and most beautiful body, or to the offspring of the same?—What is there that will conform to the genius of These States, and to all the facts?—What escape with

---

*Whitman here inserts a memorandum, a sort of self-query, to this effect: "A few characteristic words—words give us to see—(list of poets—Hindoo—Homer—Shakespeare—Pythagoras, Plato, Zoroaster, Menu, Socrates, Sesostris, Christ). Improve this."—H.T.

perfect freedom, without affectation, from the shoals of Johns, Peters, Davids, Marys? Or on what happy principle, popular and fluent, could other words be prefixed or suffixed to these, to make them show who they are, what land they were born in, what government, which of The States, what genius, mark, blood, times, have coined them with strong-cut coinage?

The subtle charm of the beautiful pronunciation is not in dictionaries, grammars, marks of accent, formulas of a language, or in any laws or rules. The charm of the beautiful pronunciation of all words, of all tongues, is in perfect flexible vocal organs, and in a developed harmonious soul.—All words, spoken from these, have deeper sweeter sounds, new meanings, impossible on any less terms.—Such meanings, such sounds, continually wait in every word that exists—in these words—perhaps slumbering through years, closed from all tympans of temples, lips, brains, until that comes which has the quality patiently waiting in the words. The blank left by words wanted, but unsupplied, has sometimes an unnamably putrid cadaverous meaning. It talks louder than tongues. What a stinging taste is left in that literature and conversation where have not yet been served up by resistless consent, words to be freely used in books, rooms, at table, any where, to specifically mean the act male and female.

Likely there are other words wanted.—Of words wanted, the matter is summed up in this: When the time comes for them to represent any thing or any state of things, the words will surely follow. The lack of any words, I say again, is as historical as the existence of words. As for me, I feel a hundred realities, clearly determined in me, that words are not yet formed to represent. Men like me—also women, our counterparts, perfectly equal—will gradually get to be more and more numerous—perhaps swiftly, in shoals; then the words will also follow, in shoals.—It is the glory and superb rose-hue of the English language, any where that it favors growth as the skin does—that it can soon become, wherever that is needed, the tough skin of a superior man or woman.

The art of the use of words would be a stain, a smutch, but for the stamina of things. For in manners, poems, orations, music, friendship, authorship, what is not said is just as important as what is said, and holds just as much meaning.—Fond of men, as a living woman is—fond of women, as a living man is.

I like limber, lasting, fierce words.—I like them applied to myself—and I like them in newspapers, courts, debates, congress.—Do you suppose the liberties and the brawn of These States have to do only with delicate lady-words? with gloved gentleman-words? Bad Presidents, bad judges, bad clients, bad editors, owners of slaves, and the long ranks of Northern political suckers (robbers, traitors, suborned), monopolists, infidels, castrated persons, impotent persons, shaved persons, supplejacks, ecclesiastics, men not fond of women, women not fond of men, cry down the use of strong, cutting, beautiful, rude words. To the manly instincts of the People they will forever be welcome.

In words of names, the mouth and ear of the people show antipathy to titles, misters, handles. They love short first names abbreviated to their lips: Tom, Bill, Jack.—These are to enter into literature, and be voted for on political tickets for the great offices. Expletives, words naming the act male and female, curious words and phrases of assent or inquiry, nicknames either to persons or customs. (Many actions, many kinds of character, and many of the fashions of dress have names among two thirds of the people, that would never be understood among the remaining third, and never appear in print.)

*Factories, mills, and all the processes of hundreds of different manufacturers grow thousands of words.* Cotton, woollen, and silk goods—hemp, rope, carpets, paper—hangings, paints, roofing preparations, hardware, furniture, paper mills, the printing offices with their wonderful improvements, engraving, daguerreotyping.

This is the age of the metal Iron. *Iron, with all that it does, or that belongs to iron, or flanges from it*, results in words: from the mines they have been drawn, as the ore has been drawn.—Following the universal laws of words, these are welded together in hardy forms and characters.—They are ponderous, strong, definite, not indebted to the antique—they are iron words, wrought and cast.—I see them all good, faithful, massive, permanent words. I love well these iron words of 1856.—*Coal* has its words also, that assimilate very much with those of iron.

*Gold* of course has always its words.—The mint, the American coinage, the dollar piece, the fifty dollar or one hundred dollar piece—California, the metallic basis of banking, chemical tests of gold—all these have their words: Canada words, Yankee words, Mannahatta words, Virginia words, Florida and Alabama words, Texas words, Mexican and Nicaraguan words; California words, Ohio, Illinois, and Indiana words.

The different mechanics have different words—all, however, under a few great over—arching laws.—These are carpenter's words, mason's words, blacksmith's words, shoemaker's words, tailor's words, hatter's words, weaver's words, painter's words.

The *Farmer's words* are immense.—They are mostly old, partake of ripeness, home, the ground—have nutriment, like wheat and milk. Farm words are added to, now, by a new class of words, from the introduction of chemistry into farming, and from the introduction of numerous machines into the barn and field.

The nigger dialect furnishes hundreds of outré words, many of them adopted into the common speech of the mass of the people.—Curiously, these words show the old English instinct for wide open pronunciations, as *yallah* for yellow—*massah* for master—and for rounding off all the corners of words. The nigger dialect has hints of the future theory of the modification of all the words of the English language, for musical purposes, for a native grand opera in America, leaving the words just as they are for writing and speaking, but the same words so modified as to answer perfectly for

musical purposes, on grand and simple principles.—
Then we should have two sets of words, male and
female as they should be, in these states, both equally
understood by the people, giving a fit much-needed
medium to that passion for music, which is deeper and
purer in America than in any other land in the world.—
The music of America is to adopt the Italian method,
and expand it to vaster, simpler, far superber effects.—It
is not to be satisfied till it comprehends the people and
is comprehended by them.

Sea words, coast words, sloop words, sailor's and
boatman's words, words of ships, are numerous in
America.—One fourth of the people of these states are
aquatic—love the water, love to be near it, smell it, sail
on it, swim in it, fish, clam, trade to and fro upon it. To
be much on the water, or in constant sight of it, affects
words, the voice, the passions.—Around the markets,
among the fish-smacks, along the wharves, you hear a
thousand words, never yet printed in the repertoire of
any lexicon—words, strong words solid as logs, and
more beauty to me than any of the antique.

Words of the Laws of the Earth,
Words of the Stars, and about them,
Words of the Sun and Moon,
Words of Geology, History, Geography,
Words of Ancient Races,
Words of the Medieval Races,
Words of the progress of Religion, Law, Art,
    Government,

Words of the surface of the Earth, grass, rocks, trees,
    flowers, grains and the like,
Words of like climates,
Words of the Air and Heavens,
Words of the Birds of the air, and of insects,
Words of Animals,
Words of Men and Women—the hundreds of different
    nations, tribes, colors, and other distinctions,
Words of the Sea,
Words of Modern Leading Ideas,
Words of Modern Inventions, Discoveries, engrossing
    Themes, Pursuits,
Words of These States—the Year 1, Washington, the
    Primal Compact, the Second Compact (namely the
    Constitution)—trades, farms, wild lands, iron,
    steam, slavery, elections, California, and so forth,
Words of the Body, Senses, Limbs, Surface, Interior,
Words of dishes to eat, or of naturally produced things
    to eat,
Words of clothes,
Words of implements,
Words of furniture,
Words of all kinds of Building and Constructing,
Words of Human Physiology,
Words of Human Phrenology,
Words of Music,
Words of Feebleness, Nausea, Sickness, Ennui,
    Repugnance, and the like.

In most instances a characteristic word once used in a poem, speech, or what not, is then exhausted; he who thinks he is going to produce effects by freely using strong words, is ignorant of words. One single name belongs to one single place only—as a key-word of a book may be best used only once in the book.—A true composition in words, returns the human body, male or female—that is the most perfect composition, and shall be best-beloved by men and women, and shall last the longest, which slights no part of the body, and repeats no part of the body.—To make a perfect composition in words is more than to make the best building or machine, or the best statue, or picture.—It shall be the glory of the greatest masters to make perfect compositions in words.

As wonderful delineations of character—as the picturesque of men, women, history—these plays of Shakespeare and the rest are grand—our obligations to them are incalculable. Other facts remain to be considered—their foreignness to us in much of their spirit—the sentiment under which they were written, that caste is not to be questioned—that the nobleman is of one blood and the—

Costumes are retrospective—they rise out of the substrata of education, equality, ignorance, caste and the like. A nation that imports its costumes imports deformity.—Shall one man be afraid, or one woman be afraid, to dress in a beautiful, decorous, natural, wholesome, inexpensive manner, because many thousands dress in the reverse manner? There is this, also, about costumes—many save themselves from being exiled, and keep each other in countenance, by being alike foolish, dapper, extravagant. I see that the day is to come very soon in America when there will not be a flat level of costumes.

Probably there is this truth to be said about the Anglo-Saxon breed—that in real vocal use it has less of the words of the various phases of friendship and love than any other race, and more friendship and love. The literature, so full of love, is begotten of the old Celtic metrical romances, and of the extravagant lays of those who sang and narrated, in France, and thence in England—and of Italian extravaganzas—and all that sighing, vowing, kissing, dying, that was in songs in European literature in the sixteenth century.—Still, it seems as if this love-sickness engrafted on our literature were only a fair response and enjoyment that people nourish themselves with, after repressing their words.— The Americans, like the English, probably make love worse than any other race.—Voices follow character, and nothing is better than a superb vocalism. I think this land is covered with the weeds and chaff of literature.

California is sown thick with the names of all the little and big saints. Chase them away and substitute aboriginal names. What is the fitness—What the strange charm of aboriginal names?—Monongahela—it rolls with venison richness upon the palate. Among names to be revolutionized: that of the city of "Baltimore."

Never will I allude to the English Language or tongue without exultation. This is the tongue that spurns laws, as the greatest tongue must. It is the most capacious vital tongue of all—full of ease, definiteness and power—full of sustenance.—An enormous treasure-house, or range of treasure houses, arsenals, granary, chock full with so many contributions from the north and from the south, from Scandinavia, from Greece and Rome—from Spaniards, Italians and the French,—that its own sturdy home-dated Angles-bred words have long been outnumbered by the foreigners whom they lead—which is all good enough, and indeed must be.— America owes immeasurable respect and love to the past, and to many ancestries, for many inheritances— but of all that America has received from the past, from the mothers and fathers of laws, arts, letters, &c., by far the greatest inheritance is the English Language—so long in growing—so fitted.

All the greatness of any land, at any time, lies folded in its names.—Would I recall some particular country or age? the most ancient? the greatest?—I recall a few names—a mountain, or sierra of mountains—a sea or bay—a river—some mighty city—some deed of persons, friends or enemies,—some event, perhaps a great war, perhaps a greater peace—some time-marking and place-marking philosoph, divine person, king, bard, goddess, captain, discoverer, or the like.

—Thus does history, in all things, hang around a few names.—All men experience it, but no man ciphers it out.

What is the curious rapport of names?—I have been informed that there are people who say it is not important about names—one word is as good as another, if the designation be understood.—I say that nothing is more important than names.—Is art important? Are forms? Great clusters of nomenclature in a land (needed in American nomenclature) include appropriate names for the Months (those now used perpetuate old myths); appropriate names for the Days of the Week (those now used perpetuate Teutonic and Greek divinities); appropriate names for Persons American—men, women, and children; appropriate names for American places, cities, rivers, counties, &c.—The word county itself should be changed. Numbering the streets, as a general thing, with a few irresistible exceptions, is very good. No country can have its own poems without it have its own names.—The name of Niagara should be substituted for the St. Lawrence. Among the places that stand in need of fresh appropriate names are the great cities of St. Louis, New Orleans, St. Paul's.

The whole theory and practice of the naming of College societies must be remade on superior American principles.—The old theory and practice of classical education is to give way, and a new race of teachers is to appear.—I say we have here, now, a greater age to celebrate, greater ideas to embody, than anything ever in Greece or Rome—or in the names of Jupiters, Jehovahs, Apollos and their myths. The great proper names used in America must commemorate things belonging to America and dating thence.—Because, what is America

for?—To commemorate the old myths and the gods?—
To repeat the Mediterranean here? Or the uses and
growths of Europe here?—No;—(Nä-o-o) but to
destroy all those from the purposes of the earth, and to
erect a new earth in their place.

*All lies folded in names.* I have heard it said that
when the spirit arises that does not brook submission
and imitation, it will throw off the ultramarine names.—
That Spirit already walks the streets of the cities of
These States—I, and others, illustrate it.—I say
America, too, shall be commemorated—shall stand
rooted in the ground in names—and shall flow in the
water in names and be diffused in time, in days, in
months, in their names.—Now the days signify extinct
gods and goddesses—the months half-unknown rites
and emperors—and chronology with the rest is all for-
eign to America—all exiles and insults here.

But it is no small thing—no quick growth; not a
matter of rubbing out one word and of writing
another.—Real names never come so easily.—The
greatest cities, the greatest politics, the greatest physi-
ology and soul, the greatest orators, poets, and literati—
The best women, the freest leading men, the proudest
national character—such, and the like, are indispensable
before-hand.—Then the greatest names will follow, for
they are results—and there are no greater results in the
world.

Names are the turning point of who shall be
master.—There is so much virtue in names that a nation
which produces its own names, haughtily adheres to

them, and subordinates others to them, leads all the rest of the nations of the earth.—I also promulge that a nation which has not its own names, but begs them of other nations, has no identity, marches not in front but behind.

Names are a test of the esthetic and of spirituality.—A delicate subtle something there is in the right name—an undemonstrable nourishment that exhilarates the soul. Masses of men, unaware what they like, lazily inquire what difference there is between one name and another.—But the few fine ears of the world decide for them also and recognize them—the masses being always as eligible as any whether they know it or not.—All that immense volumes, and more than volumes, can tell, are conveyed in the right name. The right name of a city, state, town, man, or woman, is a perpetual feast to the esthetic and moral nature.

Names of Newspapers. What has such a name as the Ægis, The Mercury, The Herald, to do in America?

Californian, Texan, New Mexican, and Arizonian names have the sense of the ecstatic monk, the cloister, the idea of miracles, and of devotees canonized after death.—They are the results of the early missionaries and the element of piety in the old Spanish character.— They have, in the same connection, a tinge of melancholy and of a curious freedom from roughness and money-making. Such names stand strangely in California. What do such names know of democracy,— of the hunt for the gold leads and the nugget or of the religion that is scorn and negation?

American writers are to show far more freedom in the use of words.—Ten thousand native idiomatic words are growing, or are to-day already grown, out of which vast numbers could be used by American writers, with meaning and effect—words that would be welcomed by the nation, being of the national blood—words that would give that taste of identity and locality which is so dear in literature.

# Walt Whitman in Camden

It is not a little difficult to write an article about Walt Whitman's *home*, for it was humorously said by himself, not long ago, that he had all his life possessed a home only in the sense that a ship possesses one. Hardly, indeed, till the year 1884 could he be called the occupant of such a definite place, even the kind of one I shall presently describe. To illustrate his own half-jocular remark as just given, and to jot down a few facts about the poet in Camden during the last sixteen years, and about his present home, is my only purpose in this article. I have decided to steer clear of any criticism of *Leaves of Grass*, and confine myself to his condition and a brief outline of his personal history. I should also like to dwell a moment on what may be called the peculiar outfit or schooling he has chosen, to fulfil his mission as poet, according to his own ideal.

In the observation of the drama of human nature— if, indeed, "all the world's a stage"—Walt Whitman has had rare advantages as auditor, from the beginning. Several of his earlier years, embracing the age of fifteen to twenty-one, were spent in teaching country schools in Queens and Suffolk counties, New York, following the quaint old fashion of "boarding around," that is moving from house to house and farm to farm, among high and low, living a few days alternately at each, until the quarter was up, and then commencing over again. His occupation, for a long period, as printer, with frequent traveling, is to be remembered; also as carpenter. Quite a good deal of his life has been passed in boarding-houses and hotels. The three years in the Secession War of course play a marked part. He never made any long sea-voyages, but for years at one period (1846-60) went out in their boats, sometimes for a week at a time, with the New York Bay pilots, among whom he was a great favorite. In 1848-49 his location was in New Orleans, with occasional sojourns in the other Gulf States besides Louisiana. From 1865 to '73 he lived in Washington. Born in 1819, his life through childhood and as a young and middle-aged man—that is, up to 1862—was mainly spent, with a few intervals of Western and Southern jaunts, on his native Long Island, mostly in Brooklyn. At that date, aged forty-two, he went down to the field of war in Virginia, and for the three subsequent years he was actively engaged as volunteer attendant and nurse on the battlefields, to the Southern soldiers equally with the Northern, and among the wounded in the army hospitals. He was prostrated by hospital malaria and "inflammation of the veins" in 1864, but recovered. He worked "on his own hook," had indomitable strength, health, and activity, was on the move night and day, not only till the official close of the Secession struggle, but for a long time afterward, for there was a vast legacy of suffering soldiers left when the contest was over. He was permanently appointed under President Lincoln, in 1865, to a respectable office in the Attorney-General's department. (This followed his removal from a temporary clerkship in the Indian Bureau of the Interior Department. Secretary Harlan dismissed him from that post specifically for being the author of *Leaves of Grass*.) He worked on for some time in the Attorney-General's office, and was promoted, but the seeds of the hospital malaria seemed never to have been fully eradicated. He was at last struck down, quite suddenly, by a severe paralytic shock (left hemiplegia), from which—after some weeks—he was slowly recovering, when he lost by death his mother and his sister. Soon followed two additional shocks of paralysis, though slighter than the first. Summer had now commenced at Washington, and his doctor imperatively ordered the sick man an entire change of scene—the mountains or the seashore. Whitman accordingly left Washington, destined for the New Jersey or Long Island coast, but at Philadelphia found himself too ill to proceed any further. He was brought over to Camden, and has been living there ever since....

I must forbear expanding on the poet's career these fifteen years, only noting that during them (1880) occurs the final completion of *Leaves of Grass*, the object of his life. His present domicile is a little old-fashioned frame house, situated about gunshot from the Delaware River on a clean, quiet, democratic street. This "shanty," as he calls it, was purchased by the poet five years ago for $2,000—two-thirds being paid in cash. In it he occupies the second floor. I commenced by likening his home to that of a ship, and the comparison might go farther. Though larger than any vessel's cabin, Walt Whitman's room, at 328 Mickle Street, Camden, has all the rudeness, simplicity, and free-and-easy character of the quarters of some old sailor. In the good-sized, three-windowed apartment, 20 by 20 feet or over, there are a wood stove, a bare board floor of narrow planks, a comfortable bed, divers big and little boxes, a good gas lamp, two big tables, a few old uncushioned seats, and lots of pegs and hooks and shelves. Hung or tacked on the walls are pictures, those of his father, mother and sisters holding the places of honor, a portrait of a sweetheart of long ago, a large print of Osceola the Seminole chief (given to Whitman many years since by Catlin the artist), some rare old engravings by Strange, and "Banditti Regaling," by Mortimer. Heaps of books, manuscripts, memoranda, scissorings, proof-sheets, pamphlets, newspapers, old and new magazines, mysterious-looking literary bundles tied up with stout strings, lie about the floor here and there. Off against a back wall looms a mighty trunk having double locks and bands of iron—such a receptacle as comes over sea with the foreign emigrants, and you in New York may have seen hoisted by powerful tackle from the hold of some Hamburg ship.

On the main table more books, some of them evidently old-timers, a Bible, several Shakespeares—a nook devoted to translations of Homer and Aeschylus and the other Greek poets and tragedians, with Felton's and Symond's books on Greece—a collection of the works of Fauriel and Ellis on mediaeval poetry—a well-thumbed volume (his companion, off and on, for fifty years) of Walter Scott's *Border Minstrelsy*,—Tennyson, Ossian, Burns, Omar Khayyám, all miscellaneously together. Whitman's stalwart form itself luxuriates in a curious, great cane-seat chair, with posts and rungs like ship's spars; altogether the most imposing, heavy-timbered, broad-armed and broad-bottomed edifice of the kind possible. It was the Christmas gift of the young son and daughter of Thomas Donaldson, of Philadelphia, and was specially made for the poet....

(If I slightly infringe the rule laid down at the beginning, to attempt no literary criticism, I hope the reader will excuse it.) Both Walt Whitman's book and personal character need to be studied a long time and in the mass, and are not to be gauged by custom. I never knew a man who—for all he takes an absorbing interest in politics, literature, and what is called "the world"— seems to be so poised on himself alone. Dr. Drinkard, the Washington physician who attended him in his paralysis, wrote to the Philadelphia doctor into whose hands the case passed, saying among other things: "In his bodily organism, and in his constitution, tastes and habits, Whitman is the most *natural* man I have ever met." The primary foundation of the poet's character, at the same time, is certainly spiritual. Helen Price, who knew him for fifteen years, pronounces him (in Dr. Bucke's book) the most essentially religious person she ever knew. On this foundation has been built up, layer by layer, the rich, diversified, concrete experience of his life, from its earliest years. Then his aim and ideal have not been the technical literary ones. His strong individuality, willfulness, audacity, with his scorn of convention and rote, have unquestionably carried him far outside the regular metes and bounds. No wonder there are some who refuse to consider his *Leaves* as "literature." It is perhaps only because he was brought up a printer, and worked during his early years as newspaper and magazine writer, that he has put his expression in typographical form, and made a regular book of it, with lines, leaves and binding.

Of late years the poet, who will be sixty-six years old on the last day of May ensuing, has been in a state of half-paralysis. He gets out of doors regularly in fair weather, much enjoys the Delaware River, is a great frequenter of the Camden and Philadelphia Ferry, and may occasionally be seen sauntering along Chestnut or Market Street in the latter city. He has a curious sort of public sociability, talking with black and white, high and low, male and female, old and young, of all grades. He gives a word or two of friendly recognition, or a nod or smile, to each. Yet he is by no means a marked talker or logician anywhere. I know an old book-stand man who always speaks of him as Socrates. But in one respect the likeness is entirely deficient. Whitman never argues, disputes, or holds or invites a cross-questioning bout with any human being.

Through his paralysis, poverty, the embezzlement of book-agents (1874-1876), the incredible slanders and misconstructions that have followed him through life, and the quite complete failure of his book from a worldly and financial point of view, his splendid fund of personal equanimity and good spirits has remained inexhaustible, and is to-day, amid bodily helplessness and a most meagre income, more vigorous and radiant than ever.

(George Selwyn)

# Appendix: The Calamus Sequence

This is the order in which the poems appeared in the 1860 *Leaves of Grass*. The titles are those the poems had in the final 1891/2 edition. The most important changes between the first and the final versions are noted. Poems followed by an asterisk are in the present volume.

Calamus 1: In Paths Untrodden
Calamus 2: Scented Herbiage of My Breast
Calamus 3: Whoever You Are Holding Me Now in
    Hand
Calamus 4: These I Singing in Spring
Calamus 5: States!*
Calamus 6: Not Heaving from My Ribb'd Breast Only
Calamus 7: Of the Terrible Doubt of Appearances
Calamus 8: Long I Thought That Knowledge Alone
    Would Suffice*
Calamus 9: Hours Continuing Long*
Calamus 10: Recorders Ages Hence
Calamus 11: When I Heard at the Close of Day
Calamus 12: Are You the New Person Drawn toward
    Me
Calamus 13: Roots and Leaves Themselves Alone

Calamus 14: Not Heat Flames Up and Consumes
Calamus 15: Trickle Drops
Calamus 16: Who Is Now Reading This*
Calamus 17: Of Him I Love Day and Night
Calamus 18: City of Orgies
Calamus 19: Behold This Swarthy Face
Calamus 20: I Saw in Louisiana a Live Oak Growing
Calamus 21: That Music Always Round Me
Calamus 22: To a Stranger
Calamus 23: This Moment Yearning and Thoughtful
Calamus 24: I Heard it Was Charged Against Me
Calamus 25: The Prairie Grass Dividing
Calamus 26: We Two Boys Together Clinging
Calamus 27: O Living Always, Always Dying
    (In 1860, the first two lines of this poem read:
    "O Love!/ O dying—always dying!")
Calamus 28: When I Peruse the Conquer'd Fame
Calamus 29: A Glimpse
Calamus 30: A Promise to California
Calamus 31, first stanza: What Ship Puzzled at Sea?
Calamus 32, second stanza: What Place is besieged?
Calamus 33: No Labor-Saving Machine
Calamus 34: I Dream'd in a Dream
Calamus 35: To The East and the West
    (Original first line: "To You of New England."
    Emerson?)
Calamus 36: Earth, My Likeness
Calamus 37: A Leaf for Hand in Hand
Calamus 38: Fast-Anchor'd Eternal O Love
    (1860 first line read: "Primeval my love for the
    woman I love.")

Calamus 39: Sometimes with One I Love
Calamus 40: That Shadow My Likeness
Calamus 41: Among the Multitude
Calamus 42: To a Western Boy
Calamus 43: O You Whom I Often and Silently Come
Calamus 44: Here the Frailest Leaves of Me
   (1860 adds as first line: "Here my last words and most baffling.")
Calamus 45: Full of Life Now
   (1860 line 7 read "lover" instead of "comrade.")

# Notes to the Introduction

[1] Galway Kinnell, in *The Essential Whitman*, actually composed his own versions of the poems, inserting, for instance, into the 1855 text of "Song of Myself" readings from the 1856, 1860, 1867, and 1881 versions. Paraphrasing Bentley to Pope is irresistible: A very pretty poem Mr. Kinnell, but you must not call it Whitman.

[2] Two other publications contributed greatly to teaching American professors about Whitman: Matthiessen's 1950 revision of *The Oxford Book of American Verse* and Randall Jarrell's 1953 essay, "Some Lines from Whitman" (Murphy)

[3] Since these lines are unattributed on the title page of *Howl*, European student "anarchists," for whom they are favorites, often credit them to Ginsberg.

[4] For instance, William Cain, *F.O. Matthiessen and the Politics of Criticism*, 1988; Helen Vendler (ed), *Voices and Visions*, 1987; Lawrence Levine, *Highbrow/Lowbrow: The Emergence of Cultural Hierarchy in America*, 1987. In *The Heath Anthology of American Literature* (ed. Paul Lauter

*et al*, 1990), the Library of America *Complete Poetry and Collected Prose* is one of two collections of Whitman recommended to students.

[5]The most famous change in "Song of Myself" is in the third section, last stanza, second line, which in the 1855 *Leaves* read:

> As God comes a loving bedfellow and sleeps at
> my side all night and close on the peep of
> day.

In 1856, and all later editions, Whitman changed the line to read:

> As the hugging and loving bedfellow sleeps at
> my side...

I prefer the subtler revised version since the close reader of "Song of Myself" soon enough realizes that Walt's lovers are gods, as is the Whitman persona himself, as is the reader him/herself.

> Divine I am inside and out, and I make holy
> whatever I touch or am touch'd from.
> ("Song of Myself" 24)
> And what I assume you shall assume.
> ("Song of Myself" 1)

This is not the only instance in which Whitman cut a reference to the traditional, patriarchal deity even though it meant the sacrifice of an extraordinarily powerful image. An even more striking instance occurs in

an unpublished manuscript variant of "Song of Myself,"
Section 23, which includes the lines:

> I announce myself the poet of Materials and
>     exact demonstration;
> Say that Materials are just as eternal as growth,
>     the semen of God that swims the entire
>     creation.

In all Whitman's published versions, the God's semen
image is absent. Again we can only wonder at
Whitman's ruthless pruning of brilliant particulars for
the sake of embracing, holistic conception, a conception
subversive of the established order at every point. To
prefer the 1855 reading of Section 3 is to construct a
more conventional, traditional poet. But, while critics
may seek to recruit him into the retinue of the old sky
father, Whitman himself was truer to his own, more
radical intuition.

[6]Why did the reviewers fail to notice the gaps in the
Library of America *Complete Poetry and Collected Prose?*
Some of the usual explanations apply. The only really
critical review that examined in detail the editorial
methods of the first LofA volumes was Beaver's in the
*TLS* (3 June 83: 567-8). Many of the American
"reviews" were rehashes of the publisher's handouts or
essays on Whitman, which used the new volume as a
hook for the reviewer's preoccupations. By far the most
influential notice was Malcolm Cowley's (*New York
Times Book Review*, 25 Ap 82: 3, 18-19). Cowley praised

Kaplan for his inclusion of the 1855 *Leaves*, without hinting that he himself had been promoting the importance of that version for decades. It is not uncommon practice, both in the *NYTBR* and in *The New York Review of Books*, to allow a reviewer who is on one side or another of some controversial issue to conceal her/his conflict of interest and come on "objectively." Also, in *CPCP,* the tables of contents and indices are so clumsy that it is not easy to determine what the edition actually contains. One distinguished reviewer told me that he "of course assumed" that the volume contained "Respondez!.."

[7]On Sunday morning, April 28, I saw church-bound Black families stop their cars, get out and put gifts of food and money into the baskets which the students lowered from the Broadway-facing windows of the "liberated zone."

[8]This, Whitman's manifesto, is the most revised poem in *Leaves*, much of it based on the 1855 preface. It is currently fashionable among critics to prefer the 1855 prose text, which certainly proves that lots of critics suffer from tin-ear. Compare:

> The poems distilled from other poems will probably pass away. The coward will surely pass away. The expectation of the vital and great can only be satisfied by the demeanor of the vital and great. The swarms of the polished deprecating and the reflectors and the polite

float off and leave no remembrance. America
prepares with composure and goodwill for the
visitors that have sent word.

(1855 Preface)

Rhymes and rhymers pass away, poems
  distilled from poems pass away,
The swarms of reflectors and polite pass, and
  leave ashes,
Admirers, importers, obedient persons, make
  but the soil of literature,
America justifies itself, give it time, no disguise
  can deceive it or conceal from it, it is
  impassive enough,
Only towards the likes of itself will it advance
  to meet them.

("By Blue Ontario's Shore")

[9]A movement still in progress. For good examples, see:
Joseph Jay Rubin, *The Historic Whitman*, 1973; Sean
Wilentz, *Chants Democratic*, 1984; Ezra Greenspan, *Walt
Whitman and the American Reader*, 1990.

[10]"Poem of Existence" is included in the ten volumes of
the 1902 *Complete Writings*. While Eliot probably would
not have had access to them in his parents' house—he
tells that they kept *Huckleberry Finn* from him lest he be
corrupted—he would have found them on the library
shelves when he was at Harvard.

# Works Cited

Abrams, Sam. "The Betrayal of Whitman." *Exquisite Corpse*. 4. 5 (1986): 16-18.

Allen, Gay Wilson. *The New Walt Whitman Handbook*. NY: NYU UP, 1975. A useful, judicious guide to the issues and the scholarship.

Bloom, Harold. "The Real Me." *New York Review of Books* (26 Ap 86): 3-4, 6.

Burke, Kenneth. "When Lilacs Last in the Dooryard Bloom'd" in *A Century of Whitman Criticism*. Ed. Edwin H. Miller. Bloomington: Indiana UP, 1969, 291-302.

Cowley, Malcolm. "Editor's Introduction" in *Walt Whitman's Leaves of Grass: His Original Edition*. NY: Penguin/Viking. Many editions since 1959.

Greenspan, Ezra. *Walt Whitman and the American Reader*. Cambridge UP, 1990.

Holloway, Emory, ed. *The Uncollected Poetry and Prose of Walt Whitman*. 2 vols. Garden City: Doubleday, 1921. Still the most satisfactory source for many texts. Holloway was the discoverer and decipherer of many of the manuscripts, probably the greatest Whitman scholar of the century. (Usually cited as *UPP*.)

Kaplan, Justin. *Walt Whitman: A Life*. NY: Simon & Schuster, 1980.

Kenner, Hugh. "Classics by the Pound." *Harper's* (Aug 82): 71-73.

Lawrence, D.H. *Studies in Classic American Literature*. (1922). Garden City: Anchor, 1953.

Matthiessen, F.O. *American Renaissance*. NY: Oxford UP, 1941.

Miller, James Jr. *Walt Whitman*. 2nd. ed. Boston: Twayne, 1990.

Murphy, Francis. *Walt Whitman: A Critical Anthology*. Baltimore: Penguin, 1969.

Neruda, Pablo. "We Live in a Whitmanesque Age (A Speech to P.E.N.)" (1972) in Perlman, 139-141.

Perlman, Jim, *et al*, eds. *Walt Whitman: The Measure of His Song*. Minneapolis: Holy Cow, 1981. An invaluable collection of essays and poems on Whitman by 90 poets, a couple of novelists and one architect.

Reynolds, David S. *Beneath the American Renaissance*. Cambridge: Harvard UP, 1989.

Schyberg, Frederick. *Walt Whitman*. trans. E.A. Allen. NY: Columbia UP, 1951.

Teller, Walter. *Walt Whitman's Camden Conversations*. New Brunswick: Rutgers UP, 1973.

Williams, William Carlos. "An Approach to the Poem." in *English Institute Essays 1947*. NY: Columbia UP, 1948, 50-75.

Wilson, Edmund. *Letters on Literature and Politics 1912-1971*. NY: Farrar, Straus and Giroux, 1977.